S0-BZZ-528

Perspectives on the New Testament

Essays in Honor of Frank Stagg

edited by
Charles H. Talbert

MERCER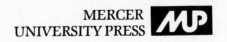
UNIVERSITY PRESS

ISBN 0-86554-152-3

BS
2395
.P47
1985

Perspectives on the New Testament
Copyright © 1985
Mercer University Press, Macon GA 31207
All rights reserved
Printed in the United States of America

All books published by Mercer University Press
are produced on acid-free paper that exceeds
the minimum standards set by the
National Historical Publications and Records Commission.

CONTENTS

PREFACE

When the editorial board of *Perspectives in Religious Studies* elected to publish a fourth issue of the journal annually beginning with Winter 1984-1985, it decided to use the extra issue to honor key Baptist scholars. This first *Festschrift* is dedicated to Frank Stagg, a Southern Baptist New Testament scholar.

A biographical sketch of Stagg's life is offered by Malcolm Tolbert, professor of New Testament at Southeastern Baptist Theological Seminary, Wake Forest, North Carolina, earlier a colleague of Stagg at New Orleans Baptist Theological Seminary. A bibliography of Stagg's works is presented by a former student of Stagg, Roger L. Omanson, professor of New Testament at Southern Baptist Theological Seminary, Louisville, Kentucky. Five areas of Stagg's special interest are represented in the five remaining articles. Professor Daryl Schmidt, Department of Religion, Texas Christian University, Fort Worth, Texas, has written an essay on Hellenistic Greek grammar. Professor George E. Rice, of the Theological Seminary at Andrews University, Berrien Springs, Michigan, has contributed an article on textual criticism of the New Testament. Hendrikus Boers, Candler School of Theology, Emory University, Atlanta, Georgia, has presented a piece on New Testament Theology. Robin Scroggs of Chicago Theological Seminary, Chicago, Illinois, has offered an essay on the New Testament and ethics. Charles H. Talbert, Department of Religion, Wake Forest University, Winston-Salem, North Carolina has written on the Holy Spirit in Pauline theology.

It is the sincere wish of the contributors to this volume and of the National Association of Baptist Professors of Religion that this issue of *Perspectives* will be useful both for study and for ministry. If so, then it will have served as a fitting tribute to the scholar we desire to honor.

CHARLES H. TALBERT, EDITOR

FRANK STAGG: TEACHING PROPHET

MALCOLM TOLBERT
SOUTHEASTERN BAPTIST THEOLOGICAL SEMINARY
WAKE FOREST, NORTH CAROLINA 27587

Friends visit Frank and Evelyn Stagg today in their home near Bay St. Louis, Mississippi, built in a beautiful setting shaded by massive oak trees that mercifully intercept and cool the rays of the Southern sun. Every grocery mart in the area sells the ingredients for the strong, aromatic coffee so integral to the daily lives of South Louisiana Cajuns. When you drop by to visit them, the Staggs immediately put on the coffee pot and pour the strong brew into your cup until met with adamant refusal. That is the way they do it in Acadia Parish, Louisiana, settled for the most part by the people of French descent, commonly called Cajuns, who give to the region its interesting cultural, gastronomic, and linguistic flavor. Visitors who know Frank Stagg well are aware that this spot is about as close to Louisiana as one can live without being a resident of that state and that the surroundings remind one daily of Acadia Parish where Frank Stagg was reared. Although the family name comes from an English ancestor, the Staggs were also Cajuns.

In a sense Frank and Evelyn Stagg had come back home in retirement—without coming all the way back. The Frank Stagg who retired on the Gulf coast of Mississippi in 1981 from his teaching position at Southern Baptist Theological Seminary in Louisville, Kentucky, is certainly not the same Frank Stagg who left his father's rice farm in 1930 to enroll in college. Yet there is a great deal of continuity in his life. The course of it was not determined by rebellion against the culture in which he was reared. He is quietly proud of his Louisiana French heritage and of his upbringing in the home of a Baptist deacon and Sunday School teacher. He expresses his positive feelings toward them in this way:

> Surely there were minuses along with the pluses in the home into which I was born and which had so much to do with my formative years, but the pluses were far more significant than the minuses. To this day, the foundations for my faith and my values are to be found in that home, housed on a rice farm in Acadia Parish in Louisiana.[1]

Most Louisiana French people were and are Roman Catholic, and so were the Staggs. Two brothers of the family, Etienne and Adolphe, began to read the Bible, however, and as a result became Baptists. Adolphe was one of the coterie of French preachers who proclaimed the gospel in their native tongue to fellow Cajuns and laid the foundation for many of the Baptist churches in South Louisiana. His name is permanently enshrined in the memory of Louisiana Baptists, for the Adolphe Stagg Association embraces churches in the area where the French pioneer preacher labored. Etienne was a rice farmer and a layman, who became the grandfather of Frank Stagg. Appropriately, if perhaps coincidentally, the grandson gave his life to a mastery of the book through which the two brothers had become evangelical Christians and became recognized as the premier New Testament scholar of his generation among Southern Baptists. No one, not even the grandfather whose life it changed so radically, has ever taken the New Testament more seriously than Frank Stagg, who has spent his entire life wrestling with it, paying the price in sweat and hours in an unrelenting quest to hear the message expressed in a language no longer spoken and directed toward a cultural context so foreign to the modern reader.

Frank was born, 20 October 1911, on his grandfather's rice farm. Since the paternal property was too small to support the new families being formed, Frank's father, Paul, moved the family five years later to a farm near Eunice, Louisiana. The Stagg children attended school and church in Eunice, making the trips on horseback or by buggy. Appropriately enough, the school, which had no need for a parking lot in those days, provided a stable for the horses ridden by the students. During his high school years Frank became aware that the family farm would not be large enough to support all the children; thus, he began to prepare for work in the business world by taking such courses as were offered in the school for that career. Subsequent to graduation his father provided a business course for him to take by correspondence. During the year following graduation from high school, however, the course of his life took a totally different turn, for he began to feel more and more that he ought to be-

---

[1]"A Continuing Pilgrimage" in *What Faith Has Meant to Me*, ed. Claude Frazier (Philadelphia: Westminster Press, 1975) 146.

come a preacher. The thought of preaching was rather terrifying, for he was by nature a shy person who could not imagine how he would manage to stand and speak to a group of people. As he wrote of the experience, "It was an unrelenting trauma that continued for a full year, a private agony shared with no one until suddenly declared openly before my home church."[2] Under the guidance of his pastor, M. E. Williamson, he began to prepare to go to Louisiana College, the only Baptist college in the state.

Frank Stagg's qualities as a leader were amply recognized by his peers in Louisiana College. An excellent student, he was intensely involved in college organizations and activities. Among other accomplishments, he served as editor of the *Wildcat*, the weekly publication of the college, president of the Baptist Student Union of Louisiana, and president of the Athenian Literary Society.

For a young man from Acadia Parish in those days of severe economic depression, graduation from high school was a genuine accomplishment, and a college education appeared to the average young person as a rather remote and almost unattainable possibility. At first Frank could hardly have entertained the idea of education beyond that lofty pinnacle. By the time he had finished his college degree, however, he had become aware that a seminary education was essential to adequate preparation for ministry. The way ahead was still beset with difficulties, primarily because of the continuing scarcity of financial resources. At the same time he felt a responsibility to remain a while longer with the church at Dodson, a quarter-time church to which he had been called as pastor in the year prior to his graduation. At the request of that congregation his home church ordained him to the ministry along with his good friend, G. Earl Guinn, on 10 September 1933. After graduation from Louisiana College in 1934, he moved to Dodson, giving an additional Sunday without an increase in salary. Some compensation was provided, however, through a member who furnished him room and board. His ministerial circuit was rounded out with service in two other quarter-time churches.

During that year of pastoral labors, the economic problem related to seminary study was solved at least in part by the offer of a scholarship, a combination of grant and loan, from Southern Baptist Seminary. This also determined that he would go to Louisville rather than the Baptist Bible Institute in New Orleans, the school that he would naturally have been inclined to attend because of its proximity.

In his junior year at Louisiana College, Frank had met the person who was to become such an integral part of his life and work, Evelyn Owen, the only daughter of an insurance executive. Born in Ruston, Louisiana, she was reared

---

[2]Ibid., 150.

in Alexandria, which lay just across the river from the college town of Pineville. She had completed the first two years of her college work at Judson College in Marion, Alabama, before matriculating in Louisiana College. On 19 August 1935, Frank and Evelyn were married, and shortly thereafter both were in classes at Southern Baptist Seminary. In those days women who were interested in the roles open to them in ministry, all of them subordinate to the male positions, were enrolled in the W.M.U. Training School. Having aborted her graduate studies in Northwestern University of Indiana in order to marry Frank, she was not going to be content with a second-class theological education. At a time when few females chose that route, her curriculum was identical with her husband's with the exception of Hebrew and preaching. The latter was obviously off limits to Southern Baptist females in the 1930s. Evelyn's seminary studies, especially in Greek and New Testament, provided her with the background she has used through the years as typist, reader, and primary editor of the many articles and books that have flowed from her husband's pen.

While at Southern Seminary, Frank was drawn to the study of the Greek New Testament. In the year prior to his enrollment in the seminary, Southern's great Greek scholar, A. T. Robertson, had died, and the senior man in the department was Hershey Davis, soon joined by E. A. McDowell. These two constituted the New Testament faculty at the time. As one might imagine, the school of A. T. Robertson took the study of the Greek New Testament very seriously. In their undergraduate work, for example, the students used the work of Tischendorf as their principal text for the course in textual criticism.

Under the tutelage of Davis and McDowell, Frank Stagg began his graduate study of the Greek New Testament in the Fall of 1938, serving as a fellow to McDowell. From the perspective of the wider field of New Testament scholarship, Southern Seminary was rather provincial in those days. The questions that scholars had been debating on the continent and in England for a century or more did not disturb the theological tranquility of the students. The main assignment for graduate majors in the Greek New Testament was to master the text. This meant that in the two-hour oral examination that preceded presentation of the thesis they had to be prepared to sight-read any portion of the Greek New Testament and talk about any of the phenomena presented by the language. This was, to be sure, a formidable enough assignment, compounded by the terror of facing professors who operated on the thesis that God had brought them to their lofty position in order to make young students aware of what they did not know.

This kind of education exerted a major influence on the shape of Frank Stagg's life. It is an understatement to say that he takes the mastery of the Greek New Testament seriously. Those of us who were his students early in his teaching career remember that for the advanced course in Greek the very idealistic young professor used as the text Robertson's *A Grammar of the Greek New Testament in the Light of Historical Research*, which contains no less than 1454 pages of often very esoteric material. His interest in the language of the text continues unabated to this day. As he himself wrote a few years ago, the Greek New Testament is his "almost daily companion."[3]

During seminary days he developed a number of friendships that were to have a profound influence on his future life. One of those friends was Duke McCall, president of two institutions in which he was later to teach. Another was Clarence Jordan, one of the genuinely great Christians of his generation, whose prophetic grasp of the gospel elevated him among his peers. Frank remembers him as the first person of his acquaintance who as a Christian had the insight and the courage to see and challenge the evils of race and war in the context of the Southern Baptist Convention.

To this point Frank had never entertained any thought other than that the pastorate would be the sphere in which he would fulfill his ministry. Work was well under way on his doctoral dissertation when a call came to assume the pastorate of the First Baptist Church of DeRidder, Louisiana, to which he had been recommended by his college Bible teacher, Professor J. E. Brakesfield. He accepted that call, and he and Evelyn moved to DeRidder in 1940.

In this first pastorate beyond his student days another element in Frank Stagg's personality came to the fore. Faced with the responsibility of preaching to people each week from the book to which he had devoted the previous years of intensive study in the seminary, he found himself having to wrestle with a question that ever since has been central in his approach to the Bible: How does the message of this book, addressed to people in a different culture and faced with different problems, relate to people living in DeRidder, Louisiana, during the war years of the 1940s? As he forcefully expressed it thirty years later, "I have no interest at all in playing in some 'theological sandbox.' Theology interests me only to the extent that it affects my existence as a person and as a servant of Christ."[4]

Frank Stagg believes that the Bible, when dealt with seriously and ethically, is profoundly related to the concerns of everyday life. "The Bible is relevant. We don't have to make it relevant, it is relevant."[5] Furthermore, he is committed to the conviction that the life and death of Jesus of Nazareth constitute the point of departure for an understanding of the God who reveals him-

---

[3]Stagg, *Polarities of Man's Existence in Biblical Perspective* (Philadelphia: Westminster Press, 1973) 12.

[4]Ibid.

[5]"Southern Baptist Theology Today: An Interview with Frank Stagg," *The Theological Educator* (Fall 1977) 34.

self in Scripture. In order to appreciate his approach to theology, you have to perceive the thoroughgoing way in which he makes Jesus the fulcrum of it, which means that the Synoptic Gospels are of central interest to him. He decries the tendency, which he sees in fundamentalists and critical scholars alike, to make Paul's letters rather than the Gospels the point of departure for dealing with central Christian issues, especially the meaning of Jesus' death.[6]

With his concern for "authentic existence" that motivated him from the very beginning, Stagg was totally repelled by the kind of theology he calls "transactionalism," so commonplace in evangelical circles in America. He criticizes "transactionalism" as an understanding of the gospel that does not touch life in any relevant way and does not bring about the kind of radical change which the gospel produced in the early followers of Jesus. In a summary statement contained in a faculty address delivered a good many years later, Stagg summarizes what he means by transactionalism: "often . . . . salvation is seen as the work of a binitarian God, compensating for inherited sin, through an event of transactional atonement, theologically described, and creedally or ritually appropriated."[7]

Stagg emphasizes that "salvation is grounded not in an external event but in God himself." Furthermore he defines salvation as becoming "an authentic human being. . . . It is for the whole man to be made whole (John 7:23) in his total ecological existence in the community of God and man and the world around him." He insists that "According to the Gospels Jesus was put to death as he engaged in saving man, not in order that he might begin to save them."[8] The Christ-event is significant in that "all that God has done in Christ is the extension and intensification of what already he was doing." The cross is important "both as a particular event at Golgotha and as belonging eternally to the nature of God."[9] This is the point of view that Stagg began to articulate in his ministry in DeRidder. If one is looking for the central theme of his entire labor as a minister, a teacher, and a writer, this is probably it.

Although he was pastor of a church in an area flooded by military people during World War II, Stagg did not engage the question of the Christian and war nearly so seriously as he was to do later. Some twenty years down the road, impelled by the Vietnamese conflict, he wrestled more intensely with this issue and came to the position on war that one notes in his more recent writings. He remembers thinking that he saw no viable alternative to American engagement in World War II, that he felt uneasy about it, and that he warned against

---

[6]Stagg, "Reassessing the Gospels," *Review and Expositor* (Spring 1981) 187ff.

[7]Stagg, "Salvation in Synoptic Tradition," *Review and Expositor* (Summer 1972) 355.

[8]Ibid., 358.

[9]Ibid., 366.

some of the obvious perils, such as the tendency of the victor to become like
the vanquished in conquest and the temptation to sanctify the American cause
by identifying it with God. The history of his engagement with the question
of war is fairly typical of the pattern of Stagg's life. He has not been one of
those exceptionally far-seeing persons, like Clarence Jordan for example, who
anticipate their contemporaries in their perception of and sensitivity to the
great issues with which humanity is to grapple many years later. He is not a
prophet in that sense. He will tell you that his own brother Paul was ahead of
him in his commitment to the struggle for racial justice. But he deserves the
title of prophet because he has always been among the first to come down on
the Christian side of the great issues of justice once they have been raised and
because of the courage with which he addresses them.

II

While Stagg was at DeRidder, his seminary friend Duke McCall became
president of Baptist Bible Institute, which under his leadership became New
Orleans Baptist Theological Seminary. Soon a need arose for a New Testament
professor, and Frank was invited to fill the post. Until that point in his life he
had never considered seriously any option other than the pastorate. The
thought of leaving the church, therefore, presented him with a difficult decision. Some of his staunchest friends and greatest admirers in the church whom
he consulted at the time loved him enough to tell him that they perceived his
principal vocation to be that of teacher. Unwilling to sway him unduly in his
search for direction, Evelyn kept her counsel as he wrestled with his decision.
Later she told him that she had felt all along that he would teach some day. He
accepted the invitation from New Orleans and on 1 January 1945 began the
first phase of his teaching career.

He brought to the teaching task the qualities already noted: a strong and
serious commitment to the centrality of the Bible for the Christian, a theology
that made the person of Jesus of Nazareth its focal point, a thorough grounding
in the study of the Greek New Testament, and a conviction that Christian truth
had to be relevant if it were to be of any value. The task of teaching gave him
the impetus and opportunity to broaden the parameters of his scholarly concern and to grapple seriously with what had been going on in the world of biblical scholarship for the previous century.

Early on, the ideas of Karl Barth, Emil Brunner, and Reinhold Niebuhr
enriched Stagg's theological perspective. In his own field he has always felt a
strong affinity for the great British scholars like T.W. Manson and C. H.
Dodd. But the scholar whom he found most attractive of all was John Baillie,
whose works, such as *The Idea of Revelation in Recent Thought* and *Our*

Knowledge of God, are always placed by Stagg at the head of any list of books that were especially meaningful to him the earlier years of his teaching ministry.

One could not seriously engage in the dialogue in biblical studies without genuine involvement with the thought of the great German scholars. Characteristically, Frank Stagg is willing to learn from anybody who has anything to say; at the same time he is committed to retaining his own integrity and individuality. Rudolf Bultmann had long been a great presence to be reckoned with and he became even more so in the 1940s and 1950s when his hermeneutical application of existentialism to the interpretation of the New Testament and his insistence on the need to demythologize it became so central. There was much in Bultmann that Stagg found attractive, especially his understanding of the contemporaneity of the gospel and his emphasis on the radical demand that it makes on the believer. Stagg's approximate contemporaries were the famous students of Bultmann who served as a corrective to the more radical thought of their master, especially with reference to his extreme skepticism about the reliability of the gospels in furnishing solid information about Jesus of Nazareth. Frank regards Ernst Käsemann, with whom he had rather close contact during a sabbatical leave at Tübingen in 1967-1968, as one of the most challenging of them all. "I may differ with him," Stagg, says, "but I find myself forced to defend my position."[10]

Coincidentally Stagg's view of the Jesus materials of the gospels has much in common with the position espoused by Günther Bornkamm in his book *Jesus of Nazareth*. When one makes due allowances for all of the legitimate findings of source, form, and redaction criticism, one must still conclude that in the gospels we possess an authentic, if impressionistic, picture of Jesus of Nazareth. We can be confident that we know the kinds of things he taught and the kinds of things he did.[11] Of course, he and Bornkamm reached this position through totally different paths. Stagg began with a rather simple and provincial understanding that claimed too much for Scripture. On the other hand, Bornkamm, along with others involved in the so-called "New Quest," had as a point of departure an extremely radical historical treatment of the Jesus materials.

Any individual who insists on the relevance of the gospel must be prepared to meet with hostility. No one is crucified for preaching for the facts of the gospel. But when someone dares to say what the gospel means in contemporary and relevant ways, hostile reaction is inevitable. No one has ever ac-

---

[10]All subsequent undocumented quotations come from an interview with Stagg by the author of this article.

[11]"Salvation in Synoptic Tradition," 356ff.

cused Frank Stagg of being anything other than an impassioned advocate of what he believes to be right and just. Passion usually provokes passion. The first of his several encounters with hostility arose over his treatment of the cross. As we have noted, he had struggled in his preaching in DeRidder with the meaning of the death of Jesus. He had rejected the idea that Jesus died to give believers a painless way out of their human situation as sinners. In so doing, of course, he had rejected the propositional concept of substitutionary atonement, the view held by many in the denomination. In response to an invitation to speak at the South Carolina conference on evangelism in March 1951, he had presented a paper, "The Rationale of the Cross." In it he subjected various traditional theories of the atonement (ransom, satisfaction, penal, substitutionary) to critical appraisal and set forth his view, concluding with this statement: "The aim of the cross is reconciliation and forgiveness. These are creative. The aim is to effect a transformation in us. God's way in Jesus confronts man; man is condemned, he fears and hates so he tries to destroy Jesus; but in this encounter man may be converted by Him who utterly refused to act for Himself—by Him who gave even His life."[12] At the request of some of his audience the paper was subsequently mimeographed and distributed to interested people. Roland Leavell, president of the New Orleans seminary, praised the paper in a faculty meeting as one of the finest works ever written on the subject. It was not long after that, however, that people committed to theories of the atonement criticized by Stagg began to raise the cries of heresy and liberalism that have followed him ever since.

The application of the gospel to the great issues of the time, so characteristic of Frank Stagg, came to full expression during the days of the civil rights struggle in the deep South. In that tumultuous period when even people who pleaded for moderation were considered radical, he consistently and clearly pointed out that the patterns that dominated in the churches as well as in society were under the judgment of God. He used his considerable skills as an interpreter of the New Testament as a force for radical change in those patterns. No student in his class when he was expounding the book of Acts could fail to understand that Stagg interpreted it from his perspective on the racial injustice in America in the twentieth century. For those of us who sat in his classes and seminars in that era, his work produced in those days, *The Book of Acts: The Early Struggle for an Unhindered Gospel*, has a significance that it can have to no other readers. We cannot read it without hearing it as the word of God directed to us, challenging the patterns of discrimination and injustice in the present. "It is possible," Stagg wrote,

that future historians may declare the irony of ironies—that in the middle of

---

[12]This unpublished paper was available to the author in mimeographed form.

the twentieth century, fight promoters and baseball managers did more for emancipating the Negro than did the churchmen. To say that these have done it for money removes none of the sting, for it is a humiliation if a pagan for money effects good which a Christian fails to effect for love. There are even evidences that segregation may make its last stand in *the churches*.[13]

People who read those words now for the first time cannot imagine the kind of hostility evoked in the 1950s and 1960s when someone translated the racial tensions of the first century into the white-black struggle of the twentieth. Because of his views on race the author was called a Communist and a liberal. Of course, his detractors never put their finger on the real cause of his prophetic concern. Frank Stagg was seeking to be a genuine follower of Jesus of Nazareth in the twentieth century.

Another of the dominant elements that make Frank Stagg what he is began to appear in those years. His loyalty to the denomination through which the gospel had come to him was tenacious. That loyalty is very understandable in view of the history of his family, which made such a notable contribution to the Baptist cause in South Louisiana. Stagg admires his forebears, especially his parents. He had a positive relationship with the church of his youth and with its pastor. He was educated in a Baptist college and seminary. His earliest commitment was to the pastorate of a Baptist church. That loyalty had been tested greatly by the time he left the New Orleans seminary for Louisville in 1964. "There were times," he said recently, "when I wondered if I would survive. However, I took the position that Southern Baptists might reject me, but I would never reject them." In a recent interview he again commented on his loyalty to Baptists.

> One reason that I am comfortable as a Baptist is that historically Baptists have made room for difference among themselves. . . . . I do feel comfortable as a Baptist as long as we can accord one another this freedom, freedom that God has given us."[14]

III

The invitation to join the faculty of his alma mater, the Southern Baptist Theological Seminary, came in 1964. Southern had recently gone though a severe crisis and had been in the process of rebuilding her faculty for some time. His college friend and colleague during the New Orleans years, Penrose St. Amant, had joined that faculty and was the dean of the School of Theology at

---

[13]Stagg, *The Book of Acts: The Early Struggle for an Unhindered Gospel* (Nashville: Broadman Press, 1955) 123-24.

[14]"Southern Baptist Theology Today: An Interview with Frank Stagg," 15-16.

the time. Stagg's old seminary classmate, Duke McCall, was the president. Obviously, there was a strong pull in that direction.

On the other hand, Stagg's loyalty to New Orleans was deep and had endured a number of severe tests. He was living in his region of the nation among the people he had known all his life. The children, Ted (Theodore), Bob (Robert), and Ginger (Virginia), had been reared in the Stagg home located on the campus of the New Orleans Seminary. Indeed, the latter two had been born in New Orleans. Furthermore, he had invested so many years of his life in the teaching task of the school and had seen it grown during those years.

There was also an imposing negative factor, however. Due to the climate engendered by the administration of the school, morale on the New Orleans campus was extremely low among many faculty, students, and graduates alike. Some of the faculty were facing the question as to how long they could remain at their posts under the circumstances. A few had already left. By that time some of us who had been Stagg's students had become his colleagues and could identify personally with the anguish attendant upon making the choice that he was called upon to make. Because of his highly developed sense of responsibility, he is not the kind of person who makes decisions like this easily or without great struggle. When he decided to accept the position at Southern, we knew something of how much it cost him to cut the ties.

In New Orleans Stagg had already published books that continue to be used as texts in various colleges and seminaries. They are also prized and often-consulted books on the shelves of hundreds of preachers faced with the daily task of interpreting the New Testament to their congregations. One was the book about Acts; another was his *Theology of the New Testament*, a key text for observing the methodology of this biblical scholar as he approaches the more systematic task of the theologian. It is also a key text for observing his own particular stance as an interpreter of the New Testament. Of course, the Stagg of today would probably write a different book, but basically it is vintage Stagg. Southern Seminary offered Frank even more of an opportunity for enlarging the sphere of his influence. As the oldest of Southern Baptist seminaries, the school enjoyed a prestige and influence associated with none of the others, an advantage to which a member of the faculty falls immediate heir. It also offered him a great outlet for his writing contributions, which were already becoming very significant. Southern had a prestigious and well-established theological journal, *The Review and Expositor*, which afforded the faculty regular opportunities for publication. Stagg was managing editor of the journal twice, serving from 1965 to 1971 and again from 1973 to 1975. Another major opportunity to make a contribution to the denomination arose when he served as editor for the New Testament section of the *Broadman Bible Commentary*, for which he also wrote the commentaries on Matthew and Philippians.

Frank Stagg's bibliography is impressive, especially to those who are aware that professors in Southern Baptist seminaries struggle against great obstacles to be productive in their writing. There is always an overload with respect to hours taught and the number of students in the classes, especially if one teaches in the biblical area. In addition the professor has the constant load of demanding committee work. In examining Stagg's bibliography, one has to remember that most of his writing was done at the expense of sleep and recreation. Among the publications coming from the press during his years at Southern, special note should be taken of the book *Polarities of Man's Existence in Biblical Perspective* (1973), for it is probably the work prized most highly by the author himself. Much of his writing was undertaken to fulfill an assignment; this book was written because Stagg wanted to write it. As he explains its thesis, "the point . . . . of the book is that we can find our authentic existence only in polar situations with their inescapable tension."[15] An example of these polar situations is seen in the perspective that human beings are creatures, distinguished from other creatures in that they were created in the image of God. It is essential, therefore, to resist the temptation to escape this tension by sinking down into creaturehood, on the one hand, or by assuming the prerogatives of God, on the other.[16] This book brings together decades of thinking about the meaning of human existence in the light of biblical insights, twin centers which dominated Stagg's development and determined to a great extent his contribution as a Christian scholar.

After he moved to Southern, the geographical area of Stagg's influence was greatly enlarged, as he had the opportunity to teach students who came from and went out to different regions of the country. Perhaps one of the most significant contributions he made was through his graduate students. Already people who completed their doctorates under his guidance in New Orleans had assumed many church and denominational posts. A number were teaching on theological faculties in this country and in other lands. That influence continued to grow through his work in the graduate programs of Southern Seminary. Some of his first students are now drawing close to retirement age, so he has had the satisfaction of seeing his labors multiplied many times over through them.

While he was teaching at Southern, new issues claimed the attention of this man who was always seeking to see the relevance of the teachings of the Bible to modern life. In the decade of the 1960s the Vietnam conflict began to assume an enormous importance in American life. For some time Stagg, like most of his contemporaries, did not focus on the American role in that sad re-

---

[15]*Polarities of Man's Existence*, 17.

[16]Ibid., 19ff.

gion. At first, the engagement of our forces there was a small cloud on a distant horizon, but before it was over it became a storm that engulfed the nation in its turbulence. Frank's intense struggle with the issue was triggered by a book critical of the American involvement in Vietnam, entitled *Vietnam: History, Documents, and Opinions of a Major World Crisis*, edited by Mavin E. Gettlemann. The book offended Frank's sense of patriotism, and his initial reaction was negative. At this point, one of the primary characteristics of this man is brought out definitively. He believes that he cannot honestly disagree with anybody until he has earned the right to do so. Many among us dare to criticize people when they have not seriously entered into dialogue with them or even read their books. Frank is not one of them. He set out to learn everything he could about that tragic region, and in the course of his reading began to be convinced that the American position was unjustified rationally and historically and that it was indefensible from any Christian point of view. His struggle with the question of that particular war led him to a negative position on the broader issue of war itself, even a conflict that might be defended rationally.

> Why is it that the church has such a love affair with war? . . . it is strange that Christians have to be reminded that one of God's commandments is against killing. One protests that men must fight lest the wicked destroy the good. . . . But there is an issue more basic. It is a pagan premise, not a Christian one, that one must live. Jesus called to himself those willing to die. In truth, his truth, it is by dying that one lives. By killing one only destroys himself.[17]

During the decade of the 1970s Frank Stagg did not neglect other issues to which many people were becoming more and more sensitive, such as the questions of hunger and poverty, the abuse of the environment, the criminal justice system (see his bibliography in the accompanying article). But in the last years of his active teaching career, along with many others in the Western world, he became especially concerned about the injustices practiced against women. Discrimination suffered by women was so ingrained in our society and so much a part of the fabric of the churches with their male-dominated ordained ministry that even thoughtful and sensitive people were not as aware of it and as aroused by it as they should have been. A glance at the title of his book *Polarities of Man's Existence in Biblical Perspective* will indicate that Frank himself was not as sensitive to the ingrained chauvinism of our language as he was to become. Again, he was usually not the first to see clearly the dimensions of an issue. But once the level of his consciousness has been

---

[17]Stagg, "Rendering to God What Belongs to God: Christian Disengagement from the World," *Journal of Church and State* 18 (1976) 229.

raised, he has distinguished himself time and again by his courage and forth-rightness in addressing it. Stagg always—instinctively, one might say—comes down on the side of the oppressed in any situation.

His special role in all the issues with which he has dealt has been as an interpreter of Scripture. He is convinced that the Christian gospel, with Jesus of Nazareth as its key, demands that the believer take his stand for the cause of justice. His understanding of the gospel thus led him once again to champion a position that was not congenial to that of many in his denomination. A great many Southern Baptists take the position that the subordination of the female to the male in the home, in society, and in the church is the correct, orthodox biblical stance, a prejudiced position that has deep historical and cultural roots. In his classroom and in other forums Stagg began to present what he saw as the correct Christian position in the light of the teachings of Scripture. In due time a book emerged, *Woman in the World of Jesus*. In this enterprise Evelyn Stagg surfaced in the role that she had occupied behind the scenes, as a partner in their common ministry. Through the years she had been happy with and found fulfillment in her role as wife, mother, and unheralded collaborator. Although she did not have the advanced technical background from which her husband approached the New Testament, she excelled in other areas and was extremely qualified to help him in the preparation of his manuscripts. For the book on women, however, she had a background and point of view which Frank did not have—after all, he was not a woman. He could empathize with women but he could not feel as they did. This work, as is true of Stagg's labors as a teacher, scholar, and writer in general, makes Jesus the central issue for the formation of the Christian conscience on the issue of discrimination against women. Concerning Jesus and women, the authors write,

> Of utmost importance is the fact that there is no tradition indicating that Jesus in any way denigrated woman as woman. In his manner, his personal relationships, and in his teachings is compelling evidence that his basic assessment of any person was in terms of personal qualities that have no sexual identity. He knew persons, some Jews and some not, some adult and some children, some men and some women. Without denying the distinctions that were real, he affirmed the personhood that was common to all.[18]

With the publication of the book Evelyn was in demand for conferences on the subject of women in the Bible as much as or, in some cases, more than her husband. Since that time they have often done such conferences together as a wife-husband team.

---

[18]Evelyn and Frank Stagg, *Woman in the World of Jesus*. (Philadelphia: Fortress Press, 1978) 143.

IV

Some time before reaching the date when he would retire from his position, the Staggs bought the house on the Mississippi Gulf Coast where they now live. For them retirement simply means that they have entered another, extremely meaningful, phase of their activity. The major difference is that they can do what they choose to do now, rather than conform to the expectations that go with a job. Invitations to teach in various schools and to lead conferences come in to a degree that was not true even during Frank's active years of teaching. The problem is that they must decide how much they want to be involved "on the circuit" and then choose among the opportunities awaiting them. At this writing, they have just returned from a year in Europe where Frank was visiting professor at the Baptist seminary in Ruschlikon. The coming year is filled with commitments to teach and lead conferences that will take him from Florida to California.

Frank Stagg continues to dedicate a great deal of his time during these years to writing. The volume on "Galatians-Romans" in the *Knox Preaching Guides* was published in 1980, after he had moved from full-time faculty responsibilities to the status of senior professor. *The Bible Speaks on Aging* came from the press in 1981. The volume to be used in 1985 in the doctrinal study promoted by the Church Training Department of the Sunday School Board on *The Doctrine of Christ* has been sent to the publisher. It is clear, therefore, that retirement can be a misleading word when used with reference to the Staggs.

When a friend visits Frank Stagg, the conversation will turn at some point to the situation faced by the Southern Baptist Convention today, especially the peril posed by the radical forces now attempting with considerable success to seize control of its institutions. He immediately lets you know that this movement threatens his denomination at the very point most precious to him, that is, in its commitment to diversity and freedom. The convention that he knew in his youth was best personified by a pastor like George W. Truett, and he had a great loyalty to it in spite of its obvious deficiencies. But he sees the forces of reaction today as representing an attempt to take the denomination in a totally different direction. What is emerging, in his words, "is so unbaptistic, so unChristian, so ignorant that I do not see how I can support that." From his point of view the Baptist distinction is expressed in the stand for freedom and not conformity. "Monolithic community is possible only under tyranny," he says, and he sees the present trend as a movement toward tyranny.

Anything that begins with the answer has to be heretical. In this case heresy is what calls itself orthodoxy. It arrogantly assumes that its understanding is final. This absolutizes human finitude as it denies fallibility. Basically, therefore, it is idolatry.

Many people would concur with the judgment of those friends from his pastorate who perceived that Frank Stagg's greatest gifts for ministry lay in the area of teaching. But as a teacher, he functioned in the noblest role available to the Christian minister, that of the prophet. In the name of Jesus of Nazareth, "whose radicality has never been approximated by the church,"[19] he engaged the issues of his time one by one: sterile, propositional theology; the patterns of racial segregation; the issues of war and peace; the economic injustices of the world; and discrimination against women. For Frank Stagg, Jesus of Nazareth is not a remote memory of the Christian community but a contemporary—a disturbing, haunting, challenging presence who invades the innermost precincts of his existence and calls him to live under the imperative of costly grace.

People around the world are proud to say that they studied under Frank Stagg. Former students who can make that claim feel that it gives them a special distinction among their peers. To be sure, occasionally there were students who, when challenged to examine ideas that they had never made their own in the dialectic of personal struggle, reacted with hostility to Stagg's teaching. For the great majority, however, he was a special kind of teacher. He did not just impart information. After all, one can read information in a book faster than a teacher can dispense it. He was a catalyst. People who came out of his classes were often different because of the experience. He gave them a model for integrity and commitment difficult to emulate, but always there to judge and challenge them. To those who took their teacher seriously, Jesus of Nazareth also became a real presence, ever out ahead of them, insistent in his call for them to explore the frontiers of authentic existence by experiencing life through dying.

---

[19]"Reassessing the Gospels," 202.

BIBLIOGRAPHY OF THEOLOGICAL WORKS BY FRANK STAGG

ROGER L. OMANSON
SOUTHERN BAPTIST THEOLOGICAL SEMINARY
LOUISVILLE, KENTUCKY 40280

BOOKS

The Book of Acts: The Early Struggle for an Unhindered Gospel. Nashville: Broadman Press, 1955.

Exploring the New Testament. Nashville: Convention Press, 1961.

New Testament Theology. Nashville: Broadman Press, 1962.

Studies in Luke's Gospel. Nashville: Convention Press, 1967.

The Holy Spirit Today. Nashville: Broadman Press, 1973.

Polarities of Man's Existence in Biblical Perspective. Philadelphia: Westminster Press, 1973.

Woman in the World of Jesus, with Evelyn Stagg. Philadelphia: Westminster Press, 1978.

Galatians and Romans. "Knox Preaching Guides," ed. John H. Hayes. Atlanta: John Knox Press, 1980.

The Bible Speaks on Aging. Nashville: Broadman Press, 1981.

CONTRIBUTIONS TO OTHER BOOKS

"He that Judgeth Me." In *More Southern Baptist Preaching*, ed. H. C. Brown, Jr., pp. 104-12. Nashville: Broadman Press, 1964.

"How I Prepare My Sermons." In *More Southern Baptist Preaching*, ed. H. C. Brown, Jr., pp. 104-106. Nashville: Broadman Press, 1964.

"What and Where is the Church?" In *What Can You Believe*? ed. David K. Alexander and C. W. Junker, pp. 27-34. Nashville: Broadman Press, 1966.

"Glossolalia in the New Testament." In *Glossolalia: Tongue Speaking in Biblical, Historical, and Psychological Perspective* by Frank Stagg, E. Glenn Hinson, and Wayne E. Oates, pp. 20-44. Nashville: Abingdon Press, 1967.

"Matthew." In *The Broadman Bible Commentary*, ed. Clifton J. Allen, vol. 8, pp. 61-253. Nashville: Broadman Press, 1969.

"Rights and Responsibilities in the Teachings of Paul." In *Emerging Patterns of Rights and Responsibilities Affecting Church and State, pp. 3-7. Washington D.C.: Baptist Joint Committee on Public Affairs, 1969.*

"Authentic Morality and Militarism." In *Proceedings of the 1970 Christian Life Commission Seminar*," pp. 45-50. Nashville: Christian Life Commission of the Southern Baptist Convention, 1970.

"Explain the Ending of the Gospel of Mark, Mark 16:17-18." *In What Did the Bible Mean*, ed. Claude A. Frazier, pp. 122-25. Nashville: Broadman Press, 1971.

"Philippians." In *The Broadman Bible Commentary*, Clifton J. Allen. pp. 178-216. Nashville: Broadman Press, 1971.

"Playing God with Other People's Minds." In *Should Preachers Play God*, ed. Claude A. Frazier, pp. 115-29. Independence: Independence Press, 1973.

"The English Bible." In *How to Understand the Bible*, by Ralph Herring, Frank Stagg, et al., pp. 148-63. Nashville: Broadman Press, 1974.

"Interpreting the Bible." In *How to Understand the Bible* by Ralph Herring, Frank Stagg, et al., pp. 49-61. Nashville: Broadman Press, 1974.

"Sources in Biblical Writings," In *How to Understand the Bible*, by Ralph Herring, Frank Stagg, et al., pp. 134-47. Nashville: Broadman Press, 1974.

"The Text and Canon of the Old Testament." In *How to Understand the Bible*, by Ralph Herring, Frank Stagg, et al., pp. 106-17. Nashville: Broadman Press, 1974.

"The Text and Canon of the New Testament." In *How to Understand the Bible*, by Ralph Herring, Frank Stagg, et al., pp. 118-33. Nashville: Broadman Press, 1974.

"A Continuing Pilgrimage." In *What Faith Has Meant to Me*, ed. Claude A. Frazier, 146-56. Philadelphia: Westminster Press, 1975.

"Adam, Christ, and Us." In *New Testament Studies: Essays in Honor of Ray Summers in His Sixty-Fifth Year*, ed. Huber L. Drumwright and Curtis Vaughan, pp. 115-36. Waco: Baylor University Press, 1975.

"Establishing a Text for Luke-Acts." In *1977 Seminar Papers, Society of Biblical Literature Book of Reports*, pp. 45-58. Missoula, Montana: Scholars Press, 1977.

"A Whole Man Made Well." In *The Struggle for Meaning*, ed. by William Powell Tuck, pp. 71-79. Valley Forge PA: Judson Press, 1977.

"Biblical Perspectives on Women" (with Evelyn Stagg). In *Findings of the Consultation on Women in Church-Related Vocations*, ed. Johnni Johnson, pp. 7-16. Nashville: Southern Baptist Convention, 1978.

"What is Truth?" In *Science, Faith and Revelation, An Approach to Christian Philosophy*, ed. Robert E. Patterson, pp. 239-60. Nashville: Broadman Press, 1979.

"Understanding Call to Ministry," In *Formation for Christian Ministry*, ed. Anne Davis and Wade Rowatt, Jr., pp. 23-38. Louisville: Review and Expositor, 1981.

"Preaching from Luke-Acts." In *Biblical Preaching: An Expositor's Treasury*, ed. James W. Cox, pp. 296-305. Philadelphia: Westminster, 1983.

"Preaching from the Sermon on the Mount." In *Biblical Preaching: An Expositor's Treasury*, ed. James W. Cox, pp. 212-29. Philadelphia: Westminster, 1983.

ENCYCLOPEDIA ARTICLE

"Women in New Testament Perspective" (with Evelyn Stagg). In *Encyclopedia of Southern Baptists*, ed. Lynn Edward May, Jr., Vol. 4, pp. 2559-60. Nashville: Broadman Press, 1982.

JOURNAL ARTICLES

"The Purpose and Message of Acts." *Review and Expositor* 44 (1947) 3-21.

"The Motif of First Corinthians." *Southwestern Journal of Theology* 3 (1960) 15-24.

"The Christology of Matthew." *Review and Expositor* 59 (1962) 457-68.

"The Farewell Discourses: John 13-17." *Review and Expositor 62 (1965) 459-72.*

"The Gospel in Biblical Usage." *Review and Expositor* 63 (1966) 5-13.

"The Holy Spirit in the New Testament." *Review and Expositor* 63 (1966) 135-47.

"The Journey Toward Jerusalem in Luke's Gospel." *Review and Expositor* 64 (1967) 499-512.

"An Analysis of the Book of James." *Review and Expositor* 66 (1969) 365-68.

"Exegetical Themes in James 1 and 2." *Review and Expositor* 66 (1969) 391-402.

"The Lord's Supper in the New Testament." *Review and Expositor* 66 (1969) 5-14.

"Orthodoxy and Orthopraxy in the Johannine Epistles." *Review and Expositor* 67 (1970) 423-32.

"The Abused Aorist." *Journal of Biblical Literature* 91 (1972) 222-31.

"Salvation in Synoptic Tradition." *Review and Expositor* 69 (1972) 355-67.

"Freedom and Moral Responsibility Without License or Legalism." *Review and Expositor* 69 (1972) 483-94.

"Introduction to Colossians." *Theological Educator* 4 (1973) 7-16.

"A Teaching Outline for Acts." *Review and Expositor* 71 (1974) 533-36.

"The Unhindered Gospel." *Review and Expositor* 71 (1974) 451-62.

"Interpreting the Book of Revelation." *Review and Expositor* 72 (1975) 331-43

"The Great Words of Romans." *Theological Educator* 7 (1976) 94-102.

"The Plight of the Jew and the Gentile in Sin: Romans 1:18-3:20." *Review and Expositor* 73 (1976) 401-13.

"Prophetic Ministry Today." *Review and Expositor* 73 (1976) 179-89.

"Rendering to Caesar What Belongs to Caesar: Christian Engagement With The World." *Journal of Church and State* 18 (1976) 95-113.

"Rendering to God What Belongs to God: Christian Disengagement From the World." *Journal of Church and State* 18 (1976) 217-32.

"Biblical Perspectives on the Single Person." *Review and Expositor* 74 (1977) 5-19.

"Southern Baptist Theology Today: An Interview," *Theological Educator* 3 (1977) 15-36.

"Textual Criticism for Luke-Acts." *Perspectives in Religious Studies* 5 (1978) 152-65.

"The Domestic Code and Final Appeal: Ephesians 5:21-6:24." *Review and Expositor* 76 (1979) 541-52.

"The New International Version: New Testament." *Review and Expositor* 76 (1979) 377-85.

"The Mind in Christ Jesus." *Review and Expositor* 77 (1980) 337-47.

"The New Testament Doctrine of the Church." *Theological Educator* 12 (1981) 42-56.

"Reassessing the Gospels." *Review and Expositor* 78 (1981) 187-203.

"Eschatology: A Southern Baptist Perspective." *Review and Expositor* 79 (1982) 381-95.

SOUTHERN BAPTIST CURRICULUM AND PERIODICAL ARTICLES

Syllabus for Study and Questions for Examination on New Testament 112: From Jesus to Paul. Nashville: Seminary Extension Department, 1954.

"Nature of the Church—Conditions of Admission." *The Baptist Student* 43 (February 1964) 53-56.

Nature of the Church—Constituents." *The Baptist Student* 43 (February 1964) 50-53.

"Nature of the Church—Individuality and Corporateness." *The Baptist Student* 43 (February 1964) 56-58.

"Church As the Body of Christ—the Ecclesia." *The Baptist Student* 43 (March 1964) 50-53.

"The Church As the Body of Christ—the Local Embodiment." *The Baptist Student* 43 (March 1964) 56-58.

"The Church As the Body of Christ—Unity and Diversity." *The Baptist Student* 43 (March 1964) 53-56.

"The Church As the Koinonia of the Spirit—Demands." *The Baptist Student*: 43 (April 1964) 54-56.

"The Church As the Koinonia of the Spirit—Dimensions." *The Baptist Student* 43 (April 1964) 52-54.

"The Church as the Koinonia of the Spirit—Primacy." *The Baptist Student* 43 (April 1964) 56-58.

"The Church in the World—the Church and the World." *The Baptist Student* 43 (May 1964) 55-57.

"The Church in the World—the Life and work of the Church." *The Baptist Student* 43 (May 1964) 52-54.

"The Church in the World—the Ministry of the Church." *The Baptist Student* 43 (May 1964) 50-52.

The Study Guide for Seminary Extension Course New Testament Theology 436 (Teacher's Edition). Nashville: Seminary Extension Department, 1964.

"1965: The Church Proclaiming." *Church Administration* 7 (February 1965) 22-24.

"Speaking in Tongues . . . A Biblical Interpretation." *The Baptist Student* 45 (May 1966) 43-45.

The Study Guide for Seminary Extension Course New Testament 202: The Gospel According to Luke. Nashville: Seminary Extension Department, 1967.

"The Radicality of Jesus Christ." *The Baptist Student* 49 (June 1970) 7-9.

"Facts About Civil Disorder." *The Baptist Program* 30 (August 1970) 30-35.

The Study Guide for Seminary Extension Course New Testament Theology 436. Nashville: Seminary Extension Department, 1971.

"The Bible Speaks on Poverty." *Outreach* 1 (July, 1971) 24-25, 30.

"The Book of Acts" *Advanced Bible Study* 2 (April-June 1972) [13 lessons on Acts].

"The Gospel of Paul in First Corinthians." *Outreach* 3 (September 1973) 30-31.

"The Gospel in Romans 1-8." *Outreach* 4 (October 1973) 30-31.

"The Gospel According to Paul Applied in Romans 12-14." *Outreach* 4 (November 1973) 42-43.

"The Radicality of Jesus Christ." *The Student* (January 1975) 8-11 (reprinted from *The Baptist Student*, June 1970).

"The Church—God's New People." *Adult Bible Teacher* 5 (April-June 1975) [13 lessons on Ephesians].

"The Kingdom of God: Freedom and Fulfillment Under the Rule of God." *Come Alive* 6 (January-March 1976) 22-33.

"Free to Be: Salvation: Becoming A Person in Christ." *Come Alive* 6 (April-June 1976) 44-55.

"First Century Demons." *Illustrator* 4 (Winter 1977) 58-60.

"The Kingdom of Heaven in Matthew." *Illustrator* (1978) 36ff.

"What We Believe About Sin." *Source* 9 (January 1979) 14-39.

"Eschatology." *One in Christ* 17 (1981) 255-270.

"The Bible Speaks on Aging." *Search* 12 (Summer 1982) 6-11.

"Humanism and A Free Society." *Report From the Capital* 37 (September 1982) 4-5.

BOOK REVIEWS

An Introduction to New Testament Textual Criticism, by J. Harold Greenlee. *Review and Expositor* 62 (Spring 1965) 230-31.

The Text of the New Testament: Its Transmission, Corruption and Restoration, by Bruce M. Metzger. *Review and Expositor* 62 (Spring 1965) 230.

Only the House of Israel? by T. W. Manson. *Review and Expositor* 62 (Spring 1965) 231.

A Beginner's Reader Grammar for New Testament Greek, by E. C. Colwell and E. W. Tune. *Review and Expositor* 62 (Fall 1965) 485-87.

The Central Message of the New Testament, by Joachim Jeremias. *Review and Expositor* 63 (Winter 1966) 98-99.

John the Baptist, by Charles H. H. Scobie. *Review and Expositor* 63 (Winter 1966) 99-100.

Bible Key Words vol. 5, ed. Gerhard Kittel. *Review and Expositor* 64 (Spring 1967) 230-31.

The Language of the New Testament, by Eugene Van Ness Goetchius. *Review and Expositor* 64 (Spring 1967) 231-34.

Broadman Comments, by Hugh R. Peterson, et al. *Review and Expositor* 64 (Summer 1967) 373-74.

The Meaning of the New Testament, by Barclay M. Newman. *Review and Expositor* 64 (Summer 1967) 381-82.

The Elements of New Testament Greek, by J. W. Wenham; *Key to the Elements of New Testament Greek*, by J. W. Wenham. *Review and Expositor* 64 (Fall 1967) 535-36.

An Exposition of the Gospel of Matthew, by Herschel H. Hobbs. *Review and Expositor* 64 (Fall 1967) 537.

The Formation of the New Testament, by Robert M. Grant. *Review and Expositor* 64 (Fall 1967) 536-37.

Luke and the Gnostics, by Charles H. Talbert. *Review and Expositor* 64 (Fall 1967) 537-38.

The Structure of Luke and Acts, by A. Q. Morton and G. H. C. MacGregor. *Review and Expositor* 64 (Fall 1967) 538-39.

The Four Translation New Testament. *Review and Expositor* 64 (Winter 1967) 84-85.

The Greek New Testament, ed. Kurt Aland, Matthew Black, Bruce M. Metzger, and Allen Wikgren. *Review and Expositor* 64 (Winter 1967) 83-84.

Concordance to the New English Bible—New Testament, comp. E. Elder. *Review and Expositor* 64 (Winter 1967) 86.

The Acts of the Apostles, by Richard B. Rackham; *The Testimony of the Evangelists*, by Simon Greenleaf; *A Historical Commentary on St. Paul's Epistle to the Galatians*, by William M. Ramsay; *Light from the Ancient East*, by Adolf Deissmann. *Review and Expositor* 65 (Winter 1968) 100-101.

Index to Periodical Literature on Christ and the Gospels, by Bruce M. Metzger. *Review and Expositor* 65 (Winter 1968) 106.

New Testament Greek Workbook, by James Arthur Walther. *Review and Expositor* 65 (Winter 1968) 107-108.

The Theological Tendency of Codex Bezae Cantabrigiensis in Acts, by Eldon Jay Epp. *Review and Expositor* 65 (Winter 1968) 101-102.

Introduction to the New Testament by Willi Marxsen. *Review and Expositor* 67 (Summer 1970) 373-74.

The Tendencies of the Synoptic Tradition, by E. P. Sanders. *Review and Expositor* 67 (Summer 1970) 375-76.

The Pattern of New Testament Truth, by George Eldon Ladd. *Review and Expositor* 67 (Fall 1970) 502-503.

More New Testament Studies, by C. H. Dodd. *Review and Expositor* 67 (Winter 1970) 101-102.

An Outline of the Theology of the New Testament, by Hans Conzelmann. *Review and Expositor* 67 (Winter 1970) 95-97.

In Search of the Historical Jesus, by Harvey K. McArthur. *Review and Expositor* 69 (Winter 1970) 102-103.

Interpreting the Gospels, by R. C. Briggs. *Review and Expositor* 67 (Winter 1970) 97-99.

The Founder of Christianity, by C. H. Dodd. *Review and Expositor* 68 (Spring 1971) 264-65.

The New Testament Bible. *Review and Expositor* 68 (Summer 1971) 400-402.

Jesus for a No-God World, by Neill Q. Hamilton. *Review and Expositor* 68 (Fall 1971) 540-41.

Studies in Methodology in Textual Criticism of the New Testament by Ernest C. Colwell. *Review and Expositor* 78 (Winter 1971) 123-24.

The Text of the New Testament: Its Transmission, Corruption, and Restoration, 2d ed., by Bruce M. Metzger. *Review and Expositor* 78 (Winter 1971) 123.

Companion to the New Testament: New English Bible, A. E. Harvey. *Review and Expositor* 69 (Spring 1972) 232-33.

New Testament Word Studies, by John Albert Bengel. 2 vols. *Review and Expositor* 69 (Spring 1972) 235.

A Parsing Guide to the Greek New Testament, by Nathan E. Han. *Review and Expositor* 69 (Spring 1972) 234.

A Future for the Historical Jesus, by Leander E. Keck. *Review and Expositor* 69 (Summer 1972) 371-73.

Gnosticism in Corinth, by Walter Schmithals. *Review and Expositor* 69 (Summer 1972) 379-81.

Jesus' Proclamation of the Kingdom of God, by Johannes Weiss. *Review and Expositor* 69 (Summer 1972) 385-86.

The Sayings of Jesus in the Churches of Paul, by David L. Dungan. *Review and Expositor* 69 (Summer 1972) 374-76.

A Commentary on the Revelation of John, by George Eldon Ladd. *Review and Expositor* 69 (Fall 1972) 525-26.

Highlights of the Book of Revelation, by George R. Beasley-Murray. *Review and Expositor* 69 (Fall 1972) 524-25.

Jesus and the Politics of Violence, by George R. Edwards. *Review and Expositor* 69 (Fall 1972) 521-22.

A Reader's Greek—English Lexicon of the New Testament, by Sakae Kubo. *Review and Expositor* 69 (Fall 1972) 526.

Reapproaching Paul, by Morton Scott Enslin. *Review and Expositor* 70 (Spring 1973) 243-44.

A Textual Commentary on the Greek New Testament, by Bruce M. Metzger. *Review and Expositor* 70 (Summer 1973) 399-400.

Eschatology in Luke, by E. Earle Ellis. *Review and Expositor* 71 (Summer 1974) 403-404.

Speaking in Tongues: Let's Talk About It, ed. Watson E. Mills. *Review and Expositor* 71 (Summer 1974) 404-406.

St. Luke: Theologian of Redemptive History, by Helmut Flender. *Review and Expositor* 71 (Fall 1974) 543.

The Theology of the New Testament According to its Major Witnesses: Jesus-Paul-John, by W. G. Kümmel. *Review and Expositor* 71 (Summer 1974) 394-95.

Trajectories Through Early Christianity, by James M. Robinson and Helmut Koester. *Review and Expositor* 71 (Summer 1974) 395-97.

Colossians: The Church's Lord and the Christian's Liberty, by Ralph P. Martin. *Review and Expositor* 71 (Winter 1974) 107.

Synopsis of the Four Gospels, ed. Kurt Aland. *Review and Expositor* 71 (Winter 1974) 110-12.

The Secret Gospel: The Discovery and Interpretation of the Secret Gospel According to Mark, by Morton Smith. *Review and Expositor* 71 (Winter 1974) 108-110.

The Gentiles and the Gentile Mission in Luke-Acts, by S. G. Wilson. *Review and Expositor* 72 (Winter 1975) 93-94.

A Reader's Greek-English Lexicon of the New Testament and A Beginner's Guide for the Translation of New Testament Greek, by Sakae Kubo. *Review and Expositor* 73 (Fall 1976) 479-80.

Milton and the Book of Revelation: The Heavenly Cycle, by Austin C. Dobbins. *Review and Expositor* 73 (Winter 1976) 77-78.

The Renaissance New Testament vol. one, by Randolph O. Yeager. *Review and Expositor* 74 (Summer 1977) 409-11.

The Gospel of Mark: The New Christian Jewish Passover Haggadah, by John Bowman. *Review and Expositor* 65 (Winter 1978) 96-98.

Anti-Semitism in the New Testament? by Samuel Sandmel. *Review and Expositor* 76 (Spring 1979) 258-61.

THE STUDY OF HELLENISTIC GREEK GRAMMAR IN THE LIGHT OF CONTEMPORARY LINGUISTICS

DARYL SCHMIDT
TEXAS CHRISTIAN UNIVERSITY
FORT WORTH, TEXAS 76129

The grammar of the language of the NT is best studied as a subset of Hellenistic Greek (HG) grammar. George B. Winer first championed this view in the first quarter of the nineteenth century. For Winer,

> As the language in which the N.T. is written is a variety of Greek, the proper object of a N.T. grammar would be fully accomplished by a systematic grammatical comparison of the N.T. language with the written Greek of the same age and of the same description.[1]

Winer argued that such a comparison reveals "a *single* syntax, which must be

---

[1] *A Treatise on the Grammar of New Testament Greek*, trans. W. F. Moulton (Edinburgh: T. & T. Clark, 1870); the first German edition was published in 1822. For an overview of the historical developments in this section, see Daryl Schmidt, *Hellenistic Greek Grammar and Noam Chomsky: Nominalizing Transformations*, SBLDS 62 (Chico CA: Scholars Press, 1981) ch.1.

recognized and exhibited in its unity."[2] He characterized that syntax as deriving from spoken Hellenistic Greek.[3]

Winer's approach, which today would be called synchronic, was based on "rational" grammar, the linguistics of the Enlightenment.[4] Gottfried Hermann had already applied rational grammar to the study of classical Greek[5] and Winer claimed that the results had "completely transformed the study of Greek" and would give a scientific basis to NT grammar.[6]

Winer described the *rational* method as one "which seeks for the explanation of all the phenomena of languages, even of their anomalies, in the modes of thought which characterise nations and individual writers." One principle of logical explanation is that "the fundamental meaning of every grammatical form (case, tense, mood), or the idea which underlay this form in the mind of the Greek nation, is exactly seized, and all the various uses of the form are deduced from this primary signification." Furthermore, Winer cautioned against choosing explanations that transgress "the laws of all human language."[7] Winer's understanding of the proper aims of a grammar thus anticipates in a remarkable way the direction taken by much of contemporary linguistics since Noam Chomsky.[8]

Winer's *Grammar* was translated into English by both British and American scholars and became the standard grammar of nineteenth-century NT scholarship. However, by the turn of the century, scholars in Germany, England, and America had begun to replace Winer's *Grammar* in response to the revolution in linguistics that had been underway since early in the century. The new comparative-historical philology, exemplified by Franz Bopp, sought to reconstruct the historical development of language by comparing the forms in kindred languages. An important impetus for applying this method to the study of the NT came with the significant discoveries of Greek papyri, which provided a vast new set of data to be analyzed at a time when the comparative grammarians had sharpened their tools for precise analysis. The attempt to provide detailed exhaustive lists of categories led to multi-volume works that

---

[2]Winer, *Treatise*, 3.

[3]Ibid., 21.

[4]John Lyons, *Introduction to Theoretical Linguistics* (Cambridge: Cambridge University, 1968) 17.

[5]Herrmann, *De emendanda ratione Graecae grammaticae* (Leipzig: Gerhard Fleischer, 1801).

[6]Winer, *Treatise*, 7. In an earlier translation (Masson, 1859) this method "accomplished a complete revolution."

[7]Ibid., 9.

[8]For a such a comparison, see Chomsky, *Cartesian Linguistics* (New York: Harper & Row, 1966) and *Language and Mind* (New York: Harcourt Brace Jovanovich, 1968) ch. 1.

accounted for all the extant forms evidenced in those texts.[9] The results of such an approach are still being published, as in Francis T. Gignac's *A Grammar of the Greek Papyri of the Roman and Byzantine Periods*, Volume I: *Phonology* (1977); Volume II: *Morphology* (1981); the volume(s) on syntax still remains to be published. In the General Introduction Gignac explicitly identifies his work with the tradition of comparative and historical studies, so that "The language of the papyri can be seen in the perspective of the history of Greek as a whole."[10]

The end of the nineteenth century had brought together both of the phenomena that frequently produce new grammars: a change in linguistic theory and the discovery of new texts. This double impetus sparked the revolution in Greek grammar that produced the three reference grammars still dominating NT studies today—Blass-Debrunner, Moulton-Howard-Turner and Robertson. These three represent the German, British and American applications of comparative-historical philology.

Friedrich Blass was a classical philologist who became editor of the third edition of Kühner's classical Greek grammar after Kühner's death in 1878. Kühner's grammar built on the comparative work of Bopp, which Blass pursued even more rigorously in the third edition of 1890.[11] When he then turned his attention to the Greek of the NT, he apologized in the preface to his mentor for not being more devoted to comparative linguistics (*Sprachforschung*) but remaining attached to classical *Philologie*. While the true linguist was most interested in the earliest *Sprachform*, Blass was writing about "a very late form of development" in the Greek language.[12] He suggested that his work belonged alongside Winer, since it was more replete with examples from the manuscripts.[13]

Moulton and Robertson both began as attempts to revise and update Winer, but both soon realized that too much had changed. James H. Moulton inherited the task from his father, who had translated and revised Winer in three editions from 1870-1882.[14] After his father's death in 1898, Moulton applied his background in classics and comparative philology to preparing a new revision of Winer. Since he was using a different approach to grammar from that

---

[9] See, for example, Edwin Mayser, *Grammatik der griechischen Papyri aus der Ptolemäerzeit* (Leipzig and Berlin, 1906-1936).

[10] Gignac, *Grammar* (Milan: Istituto Editoriale Cisalpino—La Goliardica) 1:43.

[11] *Ausführliche Grammatik der griechischen Sprache* (Hannover: Hahnsche, 1890).

[12] Kühner, *Grammatik des neutestamentlichen Griechisch* (Göttingen: Vandenhoeck und Ruprecht, 1896) iii.

[13] Ibid., vi.

[14] See note 1.

of Winer and had a significantly expanded data base in Deissmann's studies on the papyri, he acknowledged that his *Grammar* was much more than a revision of Winer.[15]

When Moulton's *Prolegomena* appeared in 1906, it was immediately hailed by James Hastings, editor of *Expository Times*: "In all future work on the New Testament it will be referred to as the close of one epoch of New Testament study and the opening of another."[16] The new epoch was marked by Moulton's reliance on Deissmann in changing his own conventional description of NT Greek from "Hebraic Greek" to "common Greek" and eventually to "Hellenistic Greek," and treating it as a spoken language, "a change in our conceptions of the subject nothing less than revolutionary."[17] The rest of the story of the Moulton *Grammar* is well-known: Moulton died before completing the next volume, and several other deaths delayed the volume on syntax until 1963 when Nigel Turner completed it and eventually added a small volume on style in 1976. Turner also succeeded in ending Moulton's revolutionary epoch, for he again was describing "the unique character of biblical Greek" and questioning "whether it was a spoken language."[18]

The American revision of Winer was begun by A. T. Robertson. In 1888 Robertson was a young assistant at Louisville's Southern Baptist Theological Seminary under John Broadus, a disciple of "the first scholar in America to make use of Bopp,"[19] when Broadus invited Robertson to join him in revising Winer. But the revision was soon abandoned and Robertson began a new grammar, because "so much progress had been made in comparative philology and historical grammar since Winer."[20] Robertson's aims were to make use of these new methods "as the true linguistic science,"[21] and his full title reveals his intent: *A Grammar of the Greek New Testament in the Light of Historical Research*. Robertson developed this tradition as Broadus's successor at Louisville (a tradition preserved by Frank Stagg).

As these three traditions were taking shape at the beginning of the century, a new revolution in linguistics was already underway, destined to become the

---

[15]James H. Moulton, *A Grammar of New Testament Greek*, vol. I: *Prolegomena* (Edinburgh: T & T. Clark, 1906) vii.

[16]*ExpT* 17 (March 1906) 245.

[17]Moulton, *Prolegomena*, 1.

[18]Moulton, *A Grammar of New Testament Greek*, vol. III: *Syntax*, by Nigel Turner (Edinburgh: T & T. Clark, 1963) 9.

[19]A. T. Robertson, *A Grammar of the Greek New Testament in the Light of Historical Research* (Nashville: Broadman, 1914) viii.

[20]Ibid., vii.

[21]Ibid., viii.

state of the art by mid-century. "Structuralist" linguistics began rather inaus-
piciously with the lecture notes of Ferdinand de Saussure, who contrasted his
approach with that of comparative philology,[22] an approach which has become
the basis for significant methodological movements in literary and biblical
studies, as variants of "structuralism."[23] De Saussure made the distinction
that comparative philology dealt with written texts diachronically, tracing historical developments, while he was interested in studying a speaker's language
synchronically, discovering the overall patterns that exist in the structure of a
language at any given time.[24]

The structuralist approach became popular in America, first among linguists such as Bloomfield, as a methodology for descriptive linguistics, then
among teachers of English grammar, using textbooks by Fries, Roberts and
Gleason, as a way of showing students how the building blocks of a sentence
fit together.[25] Robert Funk, who had given American NT scholars an English
edition of Blass-Debrunner,[26] realized that "a revolution had taken place in the
study and learning of language" and developed the potential of this approach
for analyzing and describing Greek into a three-volume *Grammar*.[27] Funk
worked out a "Parsing Code for Hellenistic Greek," presented at the 1972 SBL
meeting,[28] and his doctoral student, Lane McGaughy, applied Funk's methodology in a dissertation published that year, *Toward a Descriptive Analysis
of* εἶναι *as a Linking Verb in New Testament Greek*.[29] Despite this promising
beginning, however, structuralist linguistics has not proven to be the new dominant tradition in the study of NT Greek grammar.

One important reason for this is that a new "Revolution in Linguistics"
was simultaneously in progress, as noted in the pages of *The New York Review
of Books* in John Searle's lengthy article on Noam Chomsky.[30] Searle claimed

---

[22]de Saussure, *Cours de Linguistique Générale*, ed. Charles Bally and Albert Sechehaye
(Paris: Payot, 1916); English title: *Course in General Linguistics*, trans. Wade Baskin (New
York: McGraw-Hill, 1959).

[23]See, for example, Daniel Patte, *What is Structural Exegesis?* Guidelines to Biblical
Scholarship (Philadelphia: Fortress, 1976).

[24]See Lyons, *Theoretical Linguistics*, 45-46, 51-52.

[25]See Schmidt, *Hellenistic Greek Grammar*, 11-13.

[26]*A Greek Grammar of the New Testament and Other Early Christian Literature* (Chicago:
University of Chicago, 1961).

[27]Funk, *A Beginning-Intermediate Grammar of Hellenistic Greek* (Missoula MT: Scholars, 1973) xxiv.

[28]*SBL Seminar Papers 1972* II:315-30d.

[29]SBL Dissertation Series 6 (Missoula MT: Scholars, 1972).

[30]Searle, "Chomsky's Revolution in Linguistics," reprinted in *On Noam Chomsky: Critical Essays*, ed. Gilbert Harman (Garden City NY: Anchor, 1974) 2-33.

that, since the publication of *Syntactic Structures* in 1957, Chomsky had effected a revolution in keeping with the pattern described by Thomas Kuhn. Chomsky had constructed a new paradigm for linguistics, which completely redefined the goal of grammar. Searle characterized the prevailing descriptive linguistics as "a sort of verbal botany," whose aim was to describe and classify the observable forms of a language, but with a model of language inadequate for the task.

Chomsky offered instead a model of language that called for a grammar that would go beyond a goal of descriptive adequacy and would aim instead for explanatory adequacy, by formulating the rules which would explain all the possible sentences a language could generate. These rules were not to be formulated specifically for any one language, but derived from universal categories, so as to account for the common features of all human languages.[31]

Chomsky himself suggested that there is to be found in this criterion some of the legacy of seventeenth-century rational grammar, the very linguistic theory that began the modern era of the study of Greek grammar.[32] For whatever reason the old rational grammar was inadequate, it was not because its aims were misguided. Rather, it lacked a model of language adequate for its designs and Chomsky provided such a model.

The Chomskyan revolution pervaded all areas of linguistics, with its greatest impact on the study of syntax. While the earliest syntactical studies focused on the English language, Chomsky's transformational-generative (T-G) grammar has been applied to numerous languages. However, there have been only limited attempts to use T-G grammar on NT Greek.[33] Since NT scholarship is so dependent on linguistic-related studies, the lack of interest in T-G grammar on the part of NT scholars is noteworthy.

Two important factors have contributed to this apparent disinterest. First, as our brief look at the study of NT grammar has suggested, new traditions develop only after the results of a new linguistics revolution have been well established and are then applied to NT Greek. In the current revolution in linguistics, no one approach has emerged as the recognized successor to structuralist linguistics. At the 1979 Conference on Current Approaches to Syntax, "14 of the currently practiced approaches" were represented.[34] These approaches are by no means unrelated to one another but rather diverge at spe-

---

[31]For a summary of Chomsky's theory see Schmidt, *Hellenistic Greek Grammar*, ch. 2.

[32]See note 8.

[33]See the treatment of nominalizing transformations in Schmidt, *Hellenistic Greek Grammar*, ch. 3.

[34]*Syntax and Semantics*, vol. 13: *Current Approaches to Syntax*, ed. Edith A. Moravcsik and Jessica R. Wirth (New York: Academic Press, 1980) xiii.

cific points of contention. However, the differences among these approaches attest to the current diversity among practicing linguists. Thus there is no well-established set of results that can be directly applied to the grammar of NT Greek. Furthermore, this situation means that the literature in the field tends to be theoretical and polemical, which also makes application difficult.

A second important reason for the resistance to Chomskyan linguistics on the part of biblical scholars has been the nature of their enterprise. Biblical criticism in the twentieth century has been dominated by the historical-critical method, and one indispensable cornerstone of its foundation is traditional philology. Robert Funk, in his 1975 SBL presidential address, argued that "At the base of the historical method is philological expertise."[35] He also suggested a reason for its enduring appeal: "philological detail and certain ancillary disciplines, such as biblical archaeology, support scholarly 'objectivity,' while permitting one to evade the question of meaning."[36] On the British scene, Schuyler Brown in 1979, commenting on "Biblical Philology, Linguistics and The Problem of Method," noted that "contrasted with thirty years ago. . . . Philology and linguistics are . . . not only distinct but also in tension" and suggested that "the place of philology in Biblical studies must remain in doubt unless Biblical philologists became actively involved in the discussion of methodology."[37] Thus the dissatisfaction with traditional philology is not merely that it is outdated, but that it is an inadequate methodology for addressing questions of meaning.

It is safe to say that philologists have not led the way in such discussions. As hermeneutical questions come more to the forefront in biblical studies,[38] the need will increase for a linguistic approach to grammar that will overcome the limitations of nineteenth-century philology and restore the importance of studying NT Greek that it has not had since much earlier in this century.

In 1975 Lars Rydbeck asked, "What Happened to New Testament Greek Grammar After Albert Debrunner?" For a classical philologist like Rydbeck there is no new direction to go. His concluding appeal was for "a team effort . . . along lines similar to those of Adolf Deissmann. . . . What remains to be done is an integration of the Jewish material now available to us to balance the earlier interest in the Greek background.[39] While this would improve the descriptive adequacy of our traditional grammars, it does not acknowledge the

---

[35]Funk, "The Watershed of the American Biblical Tradition: The Chicago School, First Phase, 1892-1920," *JBL* 95 (1976) 19.

[36]Ibid., 21.

[37]*HeyJ* 20 (1979) 296-97.

[38]Note, for example, the appeal of Paul Ricoeur during the past decade.

[39]*NTS* 21 (1975) 424-27.

new agenda of twentieth-century linguistics. A similar note was registered by C. K. Barrett in his contribution to *The Expository Times* series, "Biblical Classics." Barrett rightfully chose to honor Moulton's then revolutionary *Prolegomena*. However, he began his article with a "word of appreciation" to the editor, which reflects what had become of the study of grammar by 1978: "Though my proposal, when he invited me to contribute to a series on Biblical Classics, to write on a Grammar, must have led him to fear that the circulation of *The Expository Times* would never recover from the shock, he nevertheless permitted me to go ahead." Barrett's concluding observation remains correct: "in the study of NT language 'Moulton' has not been replaced."[40] As much as this is a compliment to Moulton, it is also a comment about the current state of the art.

Despite the lack of any candidates to replace Debrunner or Moulton, there are some linguistic studies from the past decade that have advanced the understanding of Greek grammar. These studies tend to be of two different kinds: those whose starting point is a biblical text, and those that are concerned to explain a general feature of grammar. Such a distinction corresponds to the way H. A. Gleason has defined philology and linguistics: "Linguistics, at least potentially, deals with those things which are common to all texts in a given language, whereas philology deals with those things which are peculiar to specific texts."[41]

The studies of linguistic merit that are text-oriented might be called "the new philology," in that they typically either offer new explanations for old problems in the text, or raise new questions about the text. Theodore Mueller has contributed work in the former category. He uses transformations and case grammar to analyze the deep structure of difficult syntactical constructions, such as the uses of the genitive in Mark 1:4; Luke 2:14; Gal 3:2; Rom 1:17; and 1 John 4:2.[42] Studies of this sort tend to be very specific applications of earlier results achieved in linguistics, and as such make a contribution to exegesis more than to the study of grammar.

The more popular kind of new philology, if that is at all a useful label here, studies the text in units larger than the sentence, the level of syntax at which most grammatical studies end. An approach explicitly focused on paragraph

---

[40]Barrett, "Biblical Classics: IV. J. H. Moulton: A Grammar of New Testament Greek: Prolegomena," *ExpT* 90 (1978) 68-71.

[41]Gleason, "Linguistics and Philology," *On Language, Culture, and Religion: In Honor of Eugene A. Nida*, ed. M. Black and W. A. Smalley, Approaches to Semiotics 56 (The Hague: Mouton, 1974) 200.

[42]Mueller, "Observations on Some New Testament Texts Based on Generative-Transformational Grammar," *BT* 29 (1978) 117-29; "An Application of Case Grammar to Two NT Passages," *CTQ* 43 (1979) 320-25.

units is often called "discourse analysis." One such methodology with structuralist features is tagmemics. The practitioners of this approach to discourse analysis work primarily with the Summer Institute of Linguistics. The branch of the Summer Institute located in Dallas offers linguistics courses taught in conjunction with the University of Texas at Arlington. This has resulted in a number of theses and dissertations at UTA involving the tagmemics approach to discourse analysis, based mostly on the theories of Kenneth Pike and Robert Longacre.[43] Joseph Grimes, of Cornell University and the Summer Institute of Linguistics in Huntington Beach, has developed a variation that is more eclectic, using little of tagmenic terminology.[44]

Discourse analysis has also been of interest to translators working with the United Bible Societies, where Eugene Nida has maintained an eclectic approach to using linguistics models.[45] Such an eclectic approach to discourse analysis has been developed for the work of the Bible Societies by Johannes Louw.[46] This interest in discourse structure is typical of biblical studies in South Africa, as reflected in the journal *Neotestamentica*.[47] Both Nida and Louw appropriate "deep structure" features of T-G grammar in their approach to semantics, without directly confronting other issues involved in T-G theory.[48]

The various approaches that we have grouped under "the new philology" have not replaced the main stream of traditional scholarship, but seem to appeal particularly to evangelical exegetes, who have never been content with the nineteenth-century critical methods. This is especially the case with more conservative scholars. Alan F. Johnson, in his 1982 presidential address to the Evangelical Theological Society, discussed the origins of the historical-critical method in the legacy of the reformers, who sought the literal interpretation of Scripture in "the author's intention, which was for them located in the historical, philological and grammatical sense," so "they desired to use the philological tools of Greek and Hebrew . . . to aid them in their search for the

---

[43]For an overview of the theory see Linda K. Jones, "A Synopsis of Tagmemics," in *Syntax and Semantics*, vol 13: *Current Approaches to Syntax* (see note 34).

[44]Grimes, "Signals of Discourse Structure in Koine," *SBL Seminar Papers 1975*, 151-64.

[45]See, for example, Nida, "Implications of Contemporary Linguistics for Biblical Scholarship," *JBL* 91 (1972) 73-89.

[46]Louw, "Discourse Analysis and the Greek New Testament," *BT* 24 (1973) 101-18.

[47]See, for example, "The Structure of Mt 1-13: An Exploration into Discourse Analysis" and "Addendum: Discourse Analysis of the Greek Text of Mt 1-13," Neotestamentica 11 (1977).

[48]See especially J. P. Louw, *Semantics of New Testament Greek*, Semeia Studies 11 (Chico CA: Scholars Press, 1982).

literal sense of Scripture."[49] For conservative evangelicals "the literal sense of Scripture" is an ahistorical truth, making it appropriate to use methods from the synchronic side of structuralist linguistics in the philological service of exegeting timeless texts.

In contrast, traditional liberal exegesis, to the extent that it is still committed to recovering the original historical meaning of the text, needs comparative historical philology, as Robert Funk observed. This need to preserve the historical-critical methods explains our present quest, as noted by Rydbeck and Barrett, for a new Debrunner or a new Moulton.

The growing thrust in biblical scholarship toward narrative studies is loosening our bond to historically-oriented methods. As the text is allowed its rightful independent existence, apart from both author and exegete, a model of language that seeks to go beyond historically accurate description will present the paradigm needed for the study of grammar. The historical grammars already contain the data necessary for constructing an explanation of how the language works. To study the grammar of the language as a whole is to move from philological study to linguistic study in its proper sense.[50]

This kind of linguistic study can be seen in several recent dissertations in the field of linguistics that focus on Greek grammar. In the spirit of the new linguistics these studies aim to explain some part of Greek syntax, using examples from diverse, though mostly Classical, sources. Of special merit is the work of David Lightfoot in *Natural Logic and the Greek Moods: The Nature of the Subjunctive and Optative in Classical Greek.*[51] He devotes a chapter to complementation, the same topic I pursued in *Hellenistic Greek Grammar and Noam Chomsky: Nominalizing Transformations*. Lightfoot's conclusions from classical Greek are entirely consistent with my own on HG, even though he was using a somewhat different variation of T-G grammar called Generative Semantics. He studied a more extensive set of complementations, since he was able to include constructions from the classical period that were more limited in NT usage.

One such construction that Lightfoot explains more fully than any of the existing grammars is the participle as complement, traditionally called one of the supplementary (or complementary) uses. He discusses the participle as complement in situations where the infinitive also could be used as complement. The distinction can be illustrated with an example Lightfoot takes from

---

[49]Johnson, "The Historical-Critical Method: Egyptian Gold or Pagan Precipice?" *JEvTS* 26 (1983) 3-15; see 5-7.

[50]See Nida, "Implications," 73-74.

[51](The Hague, Mouton, 1975).

traditional grammar for the Greek verb *be ashamed* used with both complements.

Participle: *I am ashamed of* doing something that I do.

Infinitive: *I am ashamed to* do something that I have refrained from doing.[52]

Lightfoot finds inadequate the traditional attempts to account for this distinction on the basis of the class of verb involved. He offers an explanation that applies to all verb classes: the participle "is used only where the truth or actuality of the complement clause is presupposed to be true by the speaker or author."[53] Therefore, when a verb could have either an infinitive or a participle as its complement, the choice will reflect the presupposed truth claim of the proposition.

The traditional distinction of classical Greek, "the ptc. tended to denote facts and the infin. mere hearsay" is denied for NT Greek in Moulton-Turner and Blass-Debrunner.[54] However, Lightfoot's explanation of the distinction, if valid, should apply to NT usage as well. These pairs of examples seem to support Lightfoot's distinction.

Luke 8:46 ἔγνων δύναμιν ἐξεληλυθυῖαν ἀπ᾽ ἐμοῦ. I knew power had gone out from me.

Matt 16:3 τὸ πρόσωπον τοῦ οὐρανοῦ γινώσκετε διακρίνειν. You know how to discern the appearance of heaven.

John 7:32 ἤκουσαν οἱ φαρισαῖοι τοῦ ὄχλου γογγύζοντος. The Pharisees heard the crowd muttering.

John 12:18 ἤκουσαν τοῦτο αὐτὸν πεποιηκέναι τὸ σημεῖον. They heard that he had done this sign.

The participle in each pair (Luke 8:46; John 7:32) has a clearer presupposition to be "factual" to the speaker than does the infinitive. A pair of examples often cited from Paul also can be understood in this light:

2 Cor 8:22 ὃν ἐδοκιμάσαμεν . . . σπουδαῖον ὄντα. whom we proved . . . to be diligent.

I Thess 2:4 δεδοκιμάσμεθα ὑπὸ τοῦ θεοῦ πιστευθῆναι τὸ εὐαγγέλιον. We have been approved by God to be entrusted with the gospel.

The participle in 2 Cor 8:22 conveys that the speaker presupposes the proposition "He is diligent" to be true, where as in 1 Thess 2:4 the infinitive refrains

---

[52]Ibid., 42.

[53]Ibid., 41.

[54]Moulton, vol. 3; *Syntax*, 161; Blass-Debrunner, 215. Robertson maintains a distinction between the two, but for most verbs suggests that the participle is an adjective, rather than treating the entire construction as a complement (*Grammar*, 1122).

from such a presupposition regarding "We are entrusted with the gospel." The participle as complement (in T-G grammar, as nominalizing transformation) is most frequent in the NT with verbs of seeing (βλέπω, εἶδον, θεάομαι, θεωρέω, ὁράω), and with εὑρίσκω and ἀκούω.

Other dissertations of linguistic interest that study Greek grammar do not make a contribution at the same level as Lightfoot. Paul Karleen, in "The Syntax of the Participle in the Greek New Testament," uses the structuralist transformational theory of Zellig Harris, Chomsky's graduate school mentor.[55] Karleen's study includes the same constructions that we discussed from Lightfoot. Karleen also treats the participle as functioning alongside of the infinitive and ὅτι-constructions, all derived from transformed sentences. However, his structuralist theory provides no basis for explaining the difference when the participle is used. Veneeta Acson, in "A Diachronic View of Case-Marking Systems in Greek: A Localistic-Lexicase Analysis," uses a generative, nontransformational approach in treating "prepositions and nominal inflections as complementary case-marking elements."[56] This hybrid theory is able to preserve categories from traditional grammar and formalize them into a proper linguistic framework, thus integrating a large amount of information more systematically than in traditional grammars. As linguistic studies such as these continue to establish the logical boundaries of the grammar of Greek, legitimate options for exegesis will be made more explicit and linguistics then will be in the service of, not in competition with, philology.

---

[55](University of Pennsylvania, 1980).

[56](University of Hawaii, 1979) abstract.

IS BEZAE
A HOMOGENEOUS CODEX?

GEORGE E. RICE
ANDREWS UNIVERSITY
BERRIEN SPRINGS, MICHIGAN 49104

In a recent article, Ian M. Ellis evaluated the work that has been done on Codex Bezae over the last century.[1] Noting the contribution of Eldon J. Epp[2] to Bezan studies, Ellis observes, "Epp was able to demonstrate clearly that in the text of Acts in *D* there are clear theological tendencies discernable in the variants peculiar to Codex Bezae."[3]

In a brief statement on the relationship between the Synoptic Gospels and Acts in D, Ellis concludes (1) "the Bezan text of the Synoptic Gospels does not display the same highly distinctive characteristics as does the Bezan text of Acts," and (2) rather than "introducing his own expansions and alterations in order to convey his own particular theological bias," the scribe of D "copied from two separate sources, one—that of Acts—being a much freer text than the other."[4]

Ellis's comments on the relationship between the text of the Synoptic Gospels and Acts in Bezae will form the basis of inquiry for this study. To what extent is Ellis correct in his appraisal of the text of Bezae?

---

[1] Ian M. Ellis, "Codex Bezae and Recent Inquiry," *Irish Biblical Studies* 4 (1982) 82-100.

[2] Eldon J. Epp, *The Theological Tendency of Codex Bezae Cantabrigiensis in Acts* (Cambridge: University Press, 1966).

[3] Ellis, "Recent Inquiry," 83-84.

[4] Ibid., 86.

THE BEZAN TEXT OF MATTHEW AND LUKE

Two doctoral dissertations have addressed the text of the Synoptic Gospels in D. Michael W. Holmes has recently investigated the early editorial activity reflected in Matthew, with his fourth chapter devoted to the question of theological biases.[5] I have written on the theological tendencies found in Luke.[6] The text of Mark will be treated briefly in this essay. Thus we can make an evaluation of the Synoptic text in D and then assess Ellis's comment on the relationship between the text of the Synoptic Gospels and Acts.

I have shown in my dissertation and in several published articles[7] that the biases discovered by Epp in Acts are prevalent in Luke. After examining approximately 125 variants in Luke, I have concluded that two major themes can be seen, (1) the exaltation of Jesus and (2) an anti-Judaic bias. Three secondary themes woven in and around these two major themes can be isolated. (1) Mary, the mother of Jesus, and John the Baptist, the two dominant characters found in the first three chapters of Luke, are elevated beyond their significance in the accepted text of Luke. (2) Peter is made to stand out as "first" among the apostles, while the remaining apostles are protected from behavior that is not compatible with their position.[8] (3) Gentiles are favorably treated.

On the other hand, Holmes can find only nine variants at the most, located in chaps. 26 and 27, that reflect an anti-Judaic bias in Matthew.[9] Variants of a Christological nature that would tend to exalt Jesus are "few in number" and "relatively insignificant."[10] Examining an additional 21 variants, Holmes observes, "Even a cursory glance at these variants, however, reveals that for most of them the view that they are due to theological bias is at best a tenuous possibility only."[11] Concluding his work in the chapter on theological tendencies,

---

[5]Michael W. Holmes, "Early Editorial Activity and the Text of Codex Bezae in Matthew" (Ph.D. dissertation, Princeton University, 1984).

[6]George E. Rice, "The Alterations of Luke's Tradition by the Textual Variants in Codex Bezae" (Ph.D. dissertation, Case Western Reserve University, 1974).

[7]Rice, "Luke 3:22-38 in Codex Bezae. The Messianic King," *AUSS* 17 (1979) 203-208; "The Anti-Judaic Bias in the Western Text of the Gospel of Luke," *AUSS* 18 (1980) 51-57; "Some Further Examples of Anti-Judaic Bias in the Western Text of the Gospel of Luke," *AUSS* 18 (1980) 149-56; "The Role of the Populace in the Passion Narrative of Luke in Codex Bezae," *AUSS* 19 (1981) 147-53; "Western Non-Interpolations: A Defense of the Apostolate," in *Luke-Acts*, ed. Charles H. Talbert (New York: Crossroad Publishing, 1984) 1-16.

[8]See especially, Rice, "Non-Interpolations."

[9]Holmes, "Editorial Activity," 206-23.

[10]Ibid., 223-28.

[11]Ibid., 235.

Holmes says, "Clearly, however, Bezae in Matthew has not been affected by this bias in the same way or to the same extent as have Luke and Acts."[12]

ANTI-JUDAIC BIAS IN MARK

What Holmes found in the Bezan text of Matthew is reflected in the Bezan text of Mark. There is clear evidence of a bias lying behind a limited number of variants in the D text of Mark. Whether a bias can be isolated behind a small number of other variants in D is tenuous. We will begin our examination of those variants that show clear evidence of an anti-Judaic bias.

Anti-Judaic variants can be divided into three groups, (1) those that cast Jesus' opponents, mainly the religious leaders, in an unfavorable light; (2) those that minimize the relationship of Jesus and his followers with "Jewish institutions," such as the sabbath and tithe paying; and (3) those that intensify confrontations between Jesus and the religious authorities. Each of the above has a limited representation in Mark.

1. The first of the three groups can be seen in five clear examples. First, Mark's account of the healing of the man with the withered hand presents a sharper confrontation between Jesus and the religious leaders than does that of Matthew and Luke. Mark tells us how Jesus looked around upon his antagonists "with anger, being grieved with the obstinacy of their hearts" (3:5). The Western text, led by D, casts the religious authorities in a light that is even more unfavorable than the accepted text. The "obstinacy" (πωρώσει) of heart becomes "deadness" (νεκρώσει) of heart in D it sy[s].

The second variant in this group also appears in the context of confrontation. Jesus rebuked the religious leaders for clinging to their traditions in violation of God's law (7:13). He summed up his case against them by saying, "Thus making void the word of God through your tradition which you hand on" (7:13). "Your tradition" becomes "your foolish tradition" in D it sy[hmg], again placing the religious authorities in a bad light.

Another alteration within this pericope magnifies the hypocrisy of Jesus' opponents. Appealing to the Old Testament prophet, Jesus said, "Well did Isaiah prophesy of you hypocrites, as it is written, 'This people honors [τιμᾷ]]me with their lips, but their heart is far from me' " (vs. 6) For τιμᾷ D W a b c substitute ἀγαπᾷ ("loves"). The lips of this people speak words and phrases that express love, but the heart, the very seat of the emotion that is called love, is far from God. Instead of a unity between what the mouth speaks and the organ that represents the most tender emotions experienced by hu-

---

[12]Ibid., 236.

mans, there is a complete disparity. Their hypocrisy could not be portrayed in a more graphic way.

At Mark 12, Jesus sat opposite the offering receptacles located in the temple. Here we find the fourth variant. He was watching "how the crowd deposited money in the sacred treasury; and many of the rich were casting in much" (12:41). D changes this scene completely by omitting, "deposited money in the sacred treasury; and many rich." Bezan Mark now reads that Jesus was watching "how the crowd was casting in much." Liberality in gifts to God now belongs to the common people—"the crowd." The wealthy, that is, the rulers of the people, are not to be found in this scene of generosity. The poor widow now joins "the generous crowd" as she casts in her two small coins (12:42).

The last variant in the first group has given rise to limited discussion among commentators. With the Passover and Feast of Unleavened Bread approaching, the religious leaders were plotting how they might take Jesus by stealth and execute him (14:1). However, caution was being expressed by some in the council, μὴ ἐν τῇ ἑορτῇ, μήποτε ἔσται θόρυβος τοῦ λαοῦ ("not during the feast, lest there be an uproar of the people," (14:2). Μὴ ἔν τῇ ἑορτῇ has been understood to mean "not during the feast," or "not in the presence of the festival crowd."[13] In either case, the appeal expressed by the warning is for patience, "wait . . . until the people have returned to their homes. Then, when all is safe, they will kill Jesus!"[14]

The D text, supported by some Old Latin MSS, dramatizes the intensity of the desire to be rid of Jesus. The negative particle μή is omitted and μήποτε is moved forward to occupy its place. Concerning this alteration Cranfield says, "μήποτε ἐν τῇ ἑορτῇ ἔσται θόρυβος τοῦ λαοῦ is exclusively Western and looks like an attempt to get rid of the difficulty which the verse presents when ἐν τῇ ἑορτῇ is taken to mean 'during the feast,' " instead of "in the presence of the festival crowd."[15] Cranfield seems to miss the impact of this alteration. Instead of taking Jesus by stealth and putting him to death at some other time than during the feast, as the words of caution in the accepted text suggest, the Western text presents the leaders as plotting both a secret and immediate arrest and execution. The presence of the "festival crowd" during the Passover and Feast of Unleavened Bread only requires a secret execution—not a postponement. Thus, the Bezan text of Mark presents the lead-

---

[13]C. E. B. Cranfield, *The Gospel According to St. Mark* (Cambridge: University Press, 1959) 414; Josef Schmid, *The Gospel According to Mark*, trans. Kevin Condon (New York: Mercer Press, 1968) 247.

[14]William Hendriksen, *Exposition of the Gospel of Mark*, (Grand Rapids: Baker Book House, 1975) 555-56.

[15]Cranfield, *Gospel According to St. Mark*, 414.

ers as bent upon the death of Jesus. They will allow nothing to stand in their way—not even the sacred festivals of their religious calendar.

2. The second group of variants that reflect an anti-Judaic bias is that which attempts to free Jesus and his followers from "Jewish traditions." In Luke this is clearly seen in the variants that appear in the sabbath passages—4:16, 6:1-11, 23:56. Especially is this bias seen in the famous appendage to 6:4; where Jesus pronounces a blessing upon a man found working on the sabbath. It can also be seen in a variant that removes the obligation of tithe paying (11:42).[16] That the two variants in 6:4 and 11:42 appear in Bezae alone is of interest. This would seem to indicate that the scribe of D edited his exemplar at these verses, and they now reflect his own theological bias. It may very well be that what we see in these altered-sabbath passages is a reflection of what was happening historically in the church.

In the Bezan text of Mark, we find two places where variants of this type appear, and they involve the followers of Jesus only. The first variant appears in the "cornfield" pericope, where D it omit the following words of Jesus at 2:27, "the sabbath exists for man and not man for the sabbbath," as well as the first word of 2:28 (ὥστε). The resulting text now combines 2:27 and 28, and reads, "and I say to you, 'The Son of man is lord even of the sabbath.' " Thus any relationship between the sabbath and mankind is effectively removed.

Observations by commentators on this variant may be placed in three categories. (1) There are those who view Jesus' comment on the relationship between the sabbath and mankind as being spoken on another occasion, perhaps at the time of a miracle that was performed on the sabbath, but Mark included it here.[17] If this is correct, the Bezan text of Mark is accurate historically. (2) Vincent Taylor suggests a Western noninterpolation at this place, and expresses surprise that only a few commentators have recognized it as such.[18] (3) T. F. Glasson sees in this omission additional evidence that Matthew and Luke used a Western text of Mark as the basis for their gospels, for "we discover that the same omission occurs there; vs. 27 is absent and the word ὥστε of vs. 28."[19]

The second variant in this group appears in the context of the resurrection (16:1). Chap. 15 concludes with Mary Magdalene and Mary the mother of

---

[16]Rice, "Alterations," 188-89.

[17]Cranfield, *Gospel According to Saint Mark*, 117; Schmid, *Gospel According to Mark*, 72-73, Rudolf Schnackenburg, *The Gospel According to St. Mark* (New York: Herder and Herder, 1971) 1:48; Edward Schweizer, *The Good News According to Mark*, trans. Donald R. Madrig (Richmond: John Knox Press, 1970) 27.

[18]Vincent Taylor, *The Gospel According to St. Mark* (London: Macmillan, 1955) 218.

[19]T. F. Glasson, "Did Matthew and Luke Use a 'Western' Text of Mark," *ExpT* 55 (1944) 180.

Joses viewing the place where Jesus was laid (15:47). Chap. 16 opens with the words, "And when the sabbath was past, Mary Magdalene, and Mary mother of James and Salome, bought spices, so that they might go and anoint him." D (k) n omit "When the sabbath was past, Mary Magdalene, and Mary the mother of James, and Salome." By the addition of a temporal participle (πορευθεῖσαι), 16:1 is tied to the women named in the last verse of chap. 15. This verse now reads, "And when they had come, they bought spices. . . . " Once again, the followers of Jesus are removed from a relationship with the sabbath.

3. The third group of variants that reflect an anti-Judaic bias is found in four passages where confrontations between Jesus and the religious leaders are intensified. I will begin with the variant found at 3:21. The popularity of Jesus' ministry had brought large crowds together. The demands of their needs left no time for Jesus and the disciples to eat (3:20). Hearing the circulated report that the pressure of overwork was causing Jesus to lose his reason, certain individuals (οἱ παρ᾽ αὐτοῦ) took it upon themselves to seize him and interrupt his work (3:21). Before the impact of the variant can be weighed, the people who are οἱ παρ᾽ αὐτοῦ must be identified. Although the AV, ASV and RSV understand them to be Jesus' "friends," those who argue that the context of 3:31-35 would favor "his family" are more convincing.[20] The three Western variations that appear in this one verse can be seen more clearly if the Western text is placed in parallel with the accepted text, in this case represented by Codex B.

Mark 3:21

Codex B	Codex D
καὶ ἀκούσαντες	καὶ ὅτε ἤκουσαν περὶ αὐτοῦ
οἱ παρ᾽ αὐτοῦ	οἱ γραμματεῖν καὶ οἱ λοιποὶ
ἐξῆλθον κρατῆσαι αὐτὸν	ἐξῆλθον κρατησαῖσαι αὐτὸν
ἔλεγον γὰρ ὅτι	ἔλεγον γὰρ ὅτι
ἐξέστη	ἐξέσταται αὐτούς
And when they had heard,	And when they had heard about him,
his family	the scribes and the rest
came to seize him,	came to seize him,

---

[20]Cf. Robert G. Bratcher and Eugene A. Nida, *A Translator's Handbook on the Gospel of Mark* (Leiden: E. J. Brill, 1961) 116; F. C. Burkitt, "W and Θ: Studies in the Western Text of St. Mark," *JTS* 17 (1915) 11-12; Schmid, *Gospel According to Mark,* 81. Hendriksen, *Exposition of the Gospel of Mark*, 132, says that we just do not know who these people are.

| for they were saying,
"He is beside himself." | for they were saying that
he angered them. |

ἀκούσαντες] ὅτε ἤκουσαν, D
οἱ παρ' αὐτοῦ] περὶ αὐτοῦ οἱ γραμματεῖν καὶ οἱ λοιποί, D W it
ἐξέστη] ἐξέσταται αὐτούς D it

Cranfield sees the removal of Jesus' family from this verse as an indication of the extent to which the early church was embarrassed by this statement.[21] Hans-Werner Bartsch is correct, however, in seeing the Western reading as an attempt not only to remove an embarrassment, but also to incriminate the scribes and their colleagues[22] This attempt by the scribes in the Bezan text to seize Jesus intensifies the confrontation between them and Jesus over whose authority is used in Jesus' exorcisms.

The confrontation between Jesus and the merchants who were defiling the temple is also intensified. At 11:15, where the act of cleansing is described, we are told, "And he entered the temple and began to drive out those [τούς] who sold and those [τούς] who bought in the temple, and he overturned the tables of the money changers and the seats of those who sold pigeons." D, with a number of other MSS, omits the definite article (τούς) before ἀγοράζοντας ("those who bought"), thus indicating the buying and selling was done among the merchants. This, then, removes the worshipers who bought offerings within the courts of the temple from being the object of Jesus' wrath, and centers the wrath upon the merchants. D k now omit κατέστρεψεν ("he overturned") leaving ἤρξατο ἐκβάλλειν ("began to cast out") as the sole action of cleansing. Jesus, therefore, not only drove out "those who sold and bought in the temple," but he threw the tables of the money changers and the seats of the pigeon sellers out of the temple courts as well.

The next variant in this group appears at 14:48. The arresting party arrives at the Garden of Gethsemane to take Jesus into custody. In the accepted text, Jesus confronts them with the words, "Have you come out as [ὡς] against a robber, with swords and clubs to capture me?" D omits ὡς. Thus the attitude of the religious leaders, who sent the arresting party, is sharpened, "Have you come out against a robber . . . ?" This omission also explains why this band of men armed themselves—Jesus was considered dangerous. Thus the omission of ὡς sharpens and intensifies this confrontation.

---

[21]Taylor, *Gospel According to Saint Mark*, 134.

[22]Hans-Werner Bartsch, "Über dem Umgang der frühen Christenheit mit dem Text der Evangelien. Das Beispiel des Codex Bezae Cantabrigiensis," *NTS* 29 (1983) 170.

The last variant to be considered in this group is at 7:2, and introduces the confrontation between Jesus and the scribes and Pharisees (7:1-13) in which two other anti-Judaic alterations are found (7:6, 13). What makes this variant interesting is the division of Western witnesses between two synonyms. Verse 2 gives us the cause of the confrontation—the scribes and Pharisees "saw that some of his disciples ate with hands defiled, that is, unwashed." The element of confrontation is introduced by the addition of κατέγνωσαν ("they condemned") by D, thus setting a hostile atmosphere for the discussion that follows. The milder synonym ἐμέμψαντο ("they found fault") appears in other MSS where you would expect a Western reading (W lat sy[p],[h]), and in some MSS where Western readings are occasionally found (Θ f[1, 13] 28 565 700), as well as in some MSS that are not necessarily known for Western readings (K N 33 pm). Both words introduce hostility and lay the foundation for the intensified confrontation of the Western text (7:6, 13). D, however, seems to use the harsher word.

To summarize our findings in this section, (1) an anti-Judaic bias is present in Mark, but it is found in only eleven verses; (2) while Holmes found at least nine verses expressing an anti-Judaic bias in Matthew concentrated in chaps. 26 and 27, the eleven verses in Mark are dispersed throughout the gospel; (3) neither Matthew nor Mark show the frequency of this bias that can be seen in Luke/Acts.

CHRISTOLOGICAL ALTERATIONS

Along with an anti-Judaic bias, a second major theme appears in the Bezan text of Luke—the exaltation of Jesus. One of the outstanding examples is the change in the words spoken at Jesus' baptism by the heavenly voice, "You are my son, today I have begotten you" (3:22, D it). This direct quote from the royal Psalm 2:7 is followed by an alteration that is even more dramatic. Jesus' genealogy between Joseph, Jesus' adoptive father, and David is removed from Luke's text (3:23-31), and Matthew's genealogy of the kings is inserted in its place by D. The scribe even adds the names of three kings that were omitted by Matthew.[23] Thus Jesus is exalted as the Messianic King in the Bezan text of Luke.

Concerning this type of variant in Matthew, Holmes says, "Variants in the D text of Matthew, however, which may bear on either the person or work of Jesus are rather few in number and in terms of magnitude relatively insignif-

---

[23]Rice, "Alterations," 95-103.

icant."[24] What Holmes says of the D text in Matthew is true of the D text in Mark.

In his investigation of Acts, Epp cites 21 occasions when the D text gives the longer form of the name of Jesus, and "brings the title to its fullest expression, ὁ κύριος Ἰησοῦς Χριστός.[25] Although the Bezan text of Mark contains nothing of the scope found by Epp, there are two places where significant additions are found.

The title "Lord Jesus" (κύριος Ἰησοῦς) is found only once in accepted text of the Synoptic Gospels (Luke 24:13), except for the long ending of Mark (16:19). However, it is found fifteen times in Acts, and it appears frequently in the epistles. A survey of the passages in Acts leads one to the conclusion that the name "Lord Jesus" is an honorable title given to the resurrected Christ. In the Bezan text of Mark, (ὁ) $\overline{κς}$ $\overline{ις}$ is added twice (3:23, D it; 5:13, D pc (c) ff² (i) r¹). These two additions are interesting not only because Jesus is exalted by the use of this honorific title, but because this title is inserted into two pericopes that present Jesus' authority over demonic powers. In the Bezan text of Mark, ὁ $\overline{κς}$ $\overline{ις}$ is more than an honorific title, it becomes a symbol of power over demonic forces. Thus Jesus' authority is emphasized beyond the accepted text of Mark.

The addition of $\overline{κε}$ ("Lord") at Mark 9:22 (D G it) may be nothing more than a harmonization with Matthew 17:15, and a polite form of address ("Sir") on the part of the distraught father of the demon possessed boy. An unusual occurrence appears in Mark 5 and 6. ὁ $\overline{ιης}$ is added eight times by D and various Western allies (5:8, 19; 6:31, 34, 37, 38, 39. 48). What is unique is that Jesus' name is added five of the eight times within a span of nine verses in Mark 6. These additions, however, do not have any significance for our study.

The following variants do not necessarily exalt Jesus as do the additions of ὁ $\overline{κς}$ $\overline{ις}$, but they are Christological in nature and show an interest in Jesus. The first is an alteration in the words spoken by Jesus from the cross. In his dying agony Jesus cried out, "My God, my God, why has thou forsaken [ἐγκατέλιπες] me?" (15:34). D c (i) k change ἐγκατέλιπες to ὠνίδισας thus rendering the text, "My God, my God, why have you censured (or inveighed against) me?" Paul Glaue renders the indicative ὠνίδισας with a causative sense, "why have you permitted me to be abused?" Glaue is also impressed by Adolf von Harnack's argument that ὠνίδισας is to be seen as

---

[24]Holmes, "Editorial Activity," 224.

[25]Epp, *Theological Tendency*, 54-55.

representing the original text, with ἐγκατέλιπες being introduced through
the influence of the LXX.[26]

However, if we accept Jesus' cry of despair as an accurate quotation, the
Western ὠνίδισας may be seen as an attempt to prevent a misunderstanding.
The accepted text could lead one to conclude that Jesus had been abandoned
by God as he hung upon the cross, and, thus, result in a negative appraisal of
him. Ἐγκατέλιπες is softened to ὠνίδισας. Although Jesus is exposed to
treatment that may be interpreted as chastisement from God, it is not to be seen
as an abandonment by God.

The Bezan text of Mark shows a heightened interest in the resurrection of
Jesus, as is seen in the following series of alterations. Descending the Mount
of Transfiguration, Jesus instructed Peter, James and John to tell no one what
they had seen "until the Son of man should have risen from the dead. So they
kept the matter to themselves, questioning what the raising from the dead
meant" (Mark 9:9, 10). In the accepted text, the disciples questioned the
meaning of the resurrection in general. However, in D W f[1, 13] lat the questioning of the disciples centers on Jesus' own resurrection, "What does he mean,
'When he shall rise from the dead?' " (τί ἐστιν ὅταν ἐκ νεκρῶν ἀνάστη,
9:10).

With attention focused on Jesus' resurrection, we find an addition to Mark
concerning this resurrection in the most unlikely place. As Jesus and the disciples left the temple, one of the twelve pointed out the magnificence of the
temple structure (13:1). Jesus replied, "Do you see these buildings? There will
not be left here one stone upon another, that will not be thrown down" (13:2).
To this verse D W it add, "And in three days another shall rise up [ἀναστή-
σεται] without hands." One immediately thinks of John 2:19, "Destroy this
temple and in three days I shall raise it up." But the reading in Mark is not a
direct quote of John 2, which does not contain the phrase ἄνευ χειρῶν
("without hands"). Also, instead of John's ἐγερῶ ("I shall rise up") the
Western reading has ἀλλὸς ἀνανστήσεται ("another shall rise up"). The
verb ἀνίστημι, which is normally used for the resurrection, aids the Western
reading to integrate the sense of John 2 into Mark 13:2. The use of the middle
voice may add the thought contained in Jesus' words at John 10:18, that he has
authority to lay down his life and authority to take it up again. It seems clear
that this addition to Mark 13:2 shows an added interest in Jesus' resurrection
beyond that of the accepted text. It now becomes the fourth prediction made
by Jesus concerning his resurrection (the others are 8:31; 9:31; 10:34), and
supplies the basis for the next variant.

---

[26]Paul Glaue, "Einige Stellen, die die Bedeutung des Codex D Charakterisieren," *NovTest*
2 (1958) 314.

At Jesus' trial, false witnesses claimed, "We heard him say, 'I will destroy this temple that is made with hands, and in three days I will build [οἰκο-δομήσω] another, not made with hands' " (Mark 14:58). The accepted text of Mark gives no indication that Jesus made this statement. Cranfield observes that it is quite possible the false witnesses twisted Jesus' statement that the temple would be destroyed (Mark 13:2) into a statement that he would destroy it.[27] The prediction of Jesus' coming resurrection added to 13:2 by the Bezan text supplies what the accepted text lacks. The testimony of the witnesses is adjusted to the addition at 13:2. Instead of "I will build [οἰκοδομήσω] another," D it read, "I will raise up [ἀναστήσω] another." Thus, the false witnesses in the Western text, while quoting Jesus' statement about his coming resurrection, still misunderstand and misrepresent him.

The remaining alterations in this group are designed to verify the resurrection of Jesus. Although the text of D goes beyond 16:8 in Mark, several variants appear in those verses known as the short ending. At 16:6, the young man in the white robe who met the women at the tomb is identified as an angel in D ff². He informs the women that Jesus has risen. To emphasis the reality of the resurrection, the instructions in the accepted text to meet Jesus in Galilee are delivered to the women as a personal message from the risen Lord, that is, by the use of the first person singular. Again, these variants are best seen when placed in parallel with the accepted text.

MARK 16:7

Codex B	Codex D
ἀλλὰ ὑπάγετε	ἀλλὰ ὑπάγεται
εἴπατε τοῖς μαθηταῖς αὐτοῦ	καὶ εἴπατε τοῖς μαθηταῖς αὐτοῦ
καὶ τῷ πέτρῳ	καὶ τῷ πέτρῳ
ὅτι προάγει ὑμᾶς	ὅτι ἰδοὺ προάγω ὑμᾶς
εἰς τὴν γαλιλαίαν	εἰς τὴν γαλιλαίαν
ἐκεῖ αὐτὸν ὄψεσθε	ἐκεῖ με ὄψεσθαι
καθὼς εἶπεν ὑμῖν	καθὼς εἴρηκα ὑμεῖν
But go	But go
tell his disciples	and tell his disciples
and Peter	and Peter
that he is going before you	"Behold, I go before you
to Galilee;	to Galilee;

---

[27]Taylor, *Gospel According to St. Mark*, 442.

| there you will see him | there you will see me |
| as he told you. | as I have told you." |

add καὶ ante εἴπατε D C* 33 300 k
προάγει] ἰδοὺ προάγω, D K
αὐτὸν] με, D K
εἶπεν] εἴρηκα, D K

Thus the Bezan text of Mark verifies the reality of the resurrection through this personal message given to a divine messenger after the resurrection, and then delivered to the women.

In this section we have observed two variations in the Bezan text of Mark that exalt Jesus beyond the accepted text. The addition of ὁ $\overline{κς}$ $\overline{ις}$ to two pericopes dealing with exorcisms emphasizes the authority Jesus possesses over demonic powers. Six other variants show Christological interest in Jesus. One prevents the misunderstanding that Jesus was forsaken by his Father as he hung on the cross, the other five show an increased interest in the resurrection.

MISCELLANEOUS VARIANTS

The Bezan text of Luke treats Gentiles favorably and moves beyond the accepted text in freeing the Romans from the guilt of the crucifixion.[28] In the Bezan text of Mark, there seems to be only one alteration that gives favorable treatment to the Romans, even though it is not designed to free them from the guilt of the crucifixion. At 15:15, Pilate releases Barabbas and, having scourged Jesus, delivers him to be crucified. The reason for Pilate's action given in the accepted text, "wishing to satisfy the crowd," is removed by D ff[2] k r[1]. This alteration does not change the results of Pilate's decision, but it does cast Pilate in a different light. No longer is he the weak administrator who allows public whim to shape his decisions.

The Bezan text of Luke treats the apostles quite favorably, interceding in their behalf so their behavior will not be too far out of line with what is expected of them. Three verses in the Bezan text of Mark presents the apostles, and discipleship in general, in a favorable light. The first two deal with sacrifices and rewards. Peter, Andrew, James and John were the first of the apostles to be called by Jesus (Mk 1:16-20). When Jesus invited James and John to join him in ministry, we are told they left their father and followed him (1:20). The response on the part of Peter and Andrew in the accepted text is not as dramatic as that of James and John. They merely "left their nets" to follow

---

[28]Rice, "Alterations," 159-73.

Jesus (1:18). However, the altered text of Mark presents what some would call a harmonization with Luke 5:11. Τὰ δίκτυα ("their nets") is replaced by πάντα ("everything") in D it.

This complete sacrifice of "father" and "everything" becomes the topic of a discourse on the cost of discipleship in Mark 10. Peter raises the issue when he says, "Lo, we have left everything [πάντα] and followed you" (10:28). The alteration at 1:18 brings that verse into harmony with Peter's statement here. The alterations made in Jesus' response to Peter can be seen more clearly if we again place these verses in parallel.

Mark 10:29, 30

<table>
<tr><td>Codex B</td><td>Codex D</td></tr>
<tr><td>29ἔφη ὁ ι̅ς̅</td><td>29ἀποκρίθεις δὲ ὁ ι̅η̅ς̅</td></tr>
<tr><td>ἀμὴν λέγω ὑμῖν</td><td>ἀμὴν λέγω ὑμεῖν</td></tr>
<tr><td>οὐδείς ἐστιν ὃς ἀφῆκεν</td><td>οὐδείς ἐστιν ὃς ἀφῆκεν</td></tr>
<tr><td>οἰκίαν ἢ ἀδελφοὺς ἢ ἀδελφὰς</td><td>ἢ ἀδελφοὺς ἢ ἀδελφὰς</td></tr>
<tr><td>ἢ μητέρα ἢ πατέρα ἢ τέκνα</td><td>ἢ μητέρα ἢ τέκνα</td></tr>
<tr><td>ἢ ἀγροὺς ἕνεκεν ἐμοῦ καὶ</td><td>ἢ ἀγροὺς ἕνεκεν ἐμοῦ</td></tr>
<tr><td>τοῦ εὐαγγελίου</td><td>ἢ ἕνεκα τοῦ εὐαγγελίου</td></tr>
<tr><td>30ἐὰν μὴ λάβῃ</td><td>30ὃς ἂν μὴ λάβῃ</td></tr>
<tr><td>ἑκατονταπλασίονα νῦν ἐν</td><td>ἑκατονταπλασίονα ἐν</td></tr>
<tr><td>τῷ καιρῷ τούτῳ</td><td>τῷ καιρῷ τούτῳ</td></tr>
<tr><td></td><td>ὃς δὲ ἀφηκεν</td></tr>
<tr><td>οἰκίας καὶ ἀδελφοὺς καὶ</td><td>οἰκείαν καὶ ἀδελφὰς καὶ</td></tr>
<tr><td>ἀδελφὰς καὶ μητέρας καὶ</td><td>ἀδελφοὺς καὶ μητέρα καὶ</td></tr>
<tr><td>τέκνα καὶ ἀγροὺς</td><td>τέκνα καὶ ἀγροὺς</td></tr>
<tr><td>μετὰ διωγμῶν καὶ</td><td>μετὰ διωγμοῦ</td></tr>
<tr><td>ἐν τῷ αἰῶνι τῷ ἐρχομένῳ</td><td>ἐν τῷ αἰῶνι τῷ ἐρχομένῳ</td></tr>
<tr><td>ζωὴν αἰώνιαν</td><td>ζωὴν αἰώνιον λήμψεται</td></tr>
<tr><td>29Jesus said,
"Truly I say to you,
there is no one who has left
house or brothers or sisters
or mother or father or children
or lands, for my sake and
the gospel,
30who will not receive
a hundredfold now
in this time,</td><td>29Jesus said,
"Truly I say to you
there is no one who has left
either brothers or sisters
or mother or children
or lands, for my sake
or for the sake of the gospel,
30who will not receive
a hundredfold
in this time.
And he who forsakes</td></tr>
<tr><td>houses and brothers and
sisters and mothers and</td><td>house and sisters and
brothers and mother and</td></tr>
</table>

children and lands,	children and lands,
with persecutions, and	on the basis of persecution,
in the age to come	in the age to come
eternal life."	will receive eternal life."

<table>
<tr><td>

²⁹ἔφη] ἀποκρίθεις δὲ, D

omit οἰκίαν, D b

omit ἡ πατέρα, D a ff² k

καὶ ἕνεκεν²] ἢ ἕνεκα, D

</td><td>

³⁰ἐὰν] ὃς ἄν, D

omit νῦν, D pc a q syˢ

add ὁ δὲ ἄφηκεν ante οἰκίας , D it

ἀδελφάς ante καὶ ἀδελφούς D it

omit καί⁶, D it

add λήμψεται post αἰώνιον, D it

</td></tr>
</table>

The Bezan text divides the single unit of thought in verses 29 and 30 of the accepted text into two thought units. The accepted text says that those who have forsaken house, brothers, and others because of Jesus and the gospel will receive one hundredford now, in this time, houses, brothers, and others, with persecution, and in the coming age eternal life. The Bezan text alters this to read that those who have forsaken brothers and sisters, and others (house is omitted) because of Jesus and the gospel will receive one hundredfold in his time. However, what is contained in this one hundredfold is not spelled out as it is in the accepted text. The second unit of thought is created by the addition of ὁ δὲ ἄφηκεν ("the one who forsakes"). In this second unit the forsaking of worldly possessions is occasioned by persecution, and will be rewarded with eternal life. The result for discipleship is that those who forsake all because of Jesus and the gospel will receive one hundredfold in this life. Those who forsake all on the basis of persecution will receive eternal life. Greater weight is placed upon loyal discipleship in the face of persecution.

In the very next pericope, Jesus sets out for Jerusalem, telling his disciples that he is to be betrayed to the rulers and condemned to death (10:32-34). In light of the alteration made in 10:29-30, the omission in 10:32 takes on meaning. "And they were on the road, going up to Jerusalem, and Jesus was walking ahead of them; and they were amazed and those who followed were afraid." D with a number of other MSS (K f¹³ 28 700 1010 al a b) omit "and those who followed were afraid."

Some commentators identify two groups of followers in this verse, those who "were amazed" (the apostles), and those who "were afraid" (the remaining disciples).[29] The omission in the Western text removes fear from the hearts of Jesus' followers. They may have been amazed that he pressed on to

---

[29]Cranfield, *Gospel According to Saint Mark*, 335; Hendriksen, *Exposition of the Gospel of Mark*, 404; Schnackenburg, *Gospel According to St. Mark*, 2:51.

Jerusalem and persecution, a persecution that they were destined to share with him, but they were not afraid of it, for Jesus had just promised that those who experience persecution will receive the reward of eternal life.

Because of the desire by the Bezan text to cast the disciples in as favorable light as possible, the alterations at 14:4, 6 come as a complete surprise. While Jesus sat at table in Simon's house, a woman poured costly ointment over his head. "But there were some who said to themselves indignantly, 'Why was this ointment wasted?' . . . And they reproached her" (14:4, 5). D Θ 565 (it) identify the "some" who were indignant with what was done as "his disciples." It would then be the disciples who also reproached the woman in 14:5. Jesus responded to the criticism in 14:6 "Let her alone; why do you trouble her?" The accepted text simply introduces this sharp rebuke with, "But Jesus said." D 238 it add αὐτοῖς ("to them"). Thus the disciples who found fault with the woman are singled out for the rebuke.

CONCLUSION

At the beginning of this study, we noted two points made by Ellis concerning the relationship between the Bezan text of the Synoptic Gospels and Acts. He suggests that the Synoptic Gospels do "not display the same highly distinctive characteristics as does the Bezan text of Acts." The study of the Bezan text of Matthew and this present study of Mark indicate Ellis's observation is correct for these two books. However, as has been suggested, my study of Luke indicates that this gospel has the "highly distinctive characteristics" that are found in the Bezan text of Acts. Our present study of Mark shows that this gospel contains eleven variants that reflect an anti-Judaic bias, two that exalt Jesus, six that show a Christological interest, three show an interest in the disciples, and only one variant reading that reflects an interest in the Romans, for a total of twenty-three. All but three of these variants in the Bezan text are accompanied by one or more Western allies, and the significance of these three is marginal. In the Bezan text of Luke/Acts, the number of variants witnessed by D alone is impressive, and their presence makes a significant alteration in the accepted text. Therefore, Ellis's first point must be refined. The Bezan text of Matthew and Mark does not display the same highly distinctive characteristics as Acts, while the Bezan text of Luke does.

Ellis's second point is that rather than "introducing his own expansions and alterations in order to convey his own particular theological bias" the scribe of D "copied from two separate sources, one—that of Acts—being a much freer text than the other." Holmes's study of Matthew and our present study of Mark would seem to support Ellis's idea that at least these two Synoptics were copied from a different source than Acts. However, once again

Luke must be placed with Acts. Holmes concluded, "Clearly, however, Bezae in Matthew has not been affected by this bias in the same way or to the same extent as have Luke and Acts. Indeed, the difference is such as to at least raise the question whether Bezae is a homogeneous codex from book to book."[30] The present study of Mark adds weight to the question raised by Holmes. It does appear that Bezae is not a homogeneous codex. Although the Bezan text of Matthew and Mark do reflect some variants that may be attributed to a bias, they are insignificant in the comparison with the text of Luke/Acts.

In addition, although Ellis rejects the idea that the copier of D introduces his own expansions and alterations, when the unique readings contained in Luke/Acts are evaluated, the probability that this is exactly what has happened demands our attention.

---

[30]Holmes, "Editorial Activity," 236.

POLARITIES AT THE ROOTS OF NEW TESTAMENT THOUGHT: METHODOLOGICAL CONSIDERATIONS

HENDRIKUS BOERS
EMORY UNIVERSITY
ATLANTA, GEORGIA 30322

Frank Stagg has done his share to bring to light polarities in New Testament thinking. This paper is not a discussion of his work; it is rather another way of addressing the issues he has raised in *Polarities of Man's Existence in Biblical Perspective*,[1] particularly the section, "Salvation as Gift and Demand."

Two related matters concern me here—polarities and what lies at the roots of New Testament thought. The polarities at the roots of New Testament thinking may provide us with the means of addressing some of the most difficult problems of New Testament interpretation, such as the polarity between salvation as a gift and as a demand.

A. THOUGHT AND EXPRESSION IN NEW TESTAMENT INTERPRETATION

1. With regard to the roots of New Testament thought we will do well to

---

[1](Philadelphia: Westminster Press, 1973).

look back to the "history of religion" (*religionsgeschichtliche*) school,[2] and particularly to William Wrede's *Aufgabe und Methode der sogennannten neutestamentlichen Theologie*.[3] In reaction to those who interpreted the interrelationships among the various books of the New Testament at what he called a "literary" level—Ferdinand Christian Baur was a prime example—he pointed out that what we have in the New Testament writings are only surface manifestations of the much larger movement of the developing Christian religion, to which these writings gave only partial expression. The New Testament writers did not read each other's "books" as modern scholars do; they were not involved in a history of ideas, or in the development of doctrines, but they were participants in a living religion. With the exception of the synoptic gospels, connections between the New Testament books did not occur at the level of the actual writings, or of contacts between the authors, but at the more fundamental level of the Christian religion of which they were all part.

To illustrate: Matthew's reaffirmation of the importance of the Law—"Do not believe that I came to undo the Law and the Prophets; I did not come to undo but to fulfill" (Mt 5:17)—could have been articulated in reaction to views that had their roots in Paul's proclamation of salvation by faith without works of the Law, but may not necessarily have been a polemic against Paul himself. This does not diminish the radical difference in these two authors' understanding of what salvation in Christ meant. It dismisses, as far too simplistic, interpretations that are based on the assumption that Paul was the only one against whom Matthew could have reacted when he reasserted, against views similar to those of Paul, that the Law and obedience to it as the means of salvation remained the foundation of salvation.

Wrede recognized that it was necessary to distinguish between what is accessible to us of New Testament Christianity, in the form of its writings, and the more fundamental level of the actual religion itself, which found only limited expression in these writings. Wrede made another very important point in the same context—anticipating insights of contemporary linguistics—that New Testament authors did not operate with precisely defined concepts, such as "faith" or "flesh" in Paul, as one might expect from a modern, systematic thinker. To presuppose such a usage of terms by the "religious" writers of the

---

[2]The usual translation "history of religions" is inaccurate. Unlike the contemporary discipline, also called *Religionsgeschichte* in German, the *religionsgeschichtliche Schule* did not study religions, but the history of religion in contrast with the history of ideas. Literally, *Religionsgeschichte* is "history of religion" not "history of religions."

[3]William Wrede, *Über Aufgabe und Methode der sogenannten neutestamentlichen Theologie* (Göttingen: Vandenhoeck und Ruprecht, 1897); reprinted in Georg Strecker, *Das Problem der Theologie des Neuen Testaments* (Darmstadt: Wissenschaftliche Buchgesellschaft, 1975) 81-154; trans., "The Task and Methods of New Testament Theology," in Robert Morgan, *The Nature of New Testament Theology* (Naperville IL: Richardson, 1973) 68-116.

New Testament is to attribute to them a systematic way of thinking that was foreign to them. Terms such as "faith" and "flesh" should be considered in the context of their usage by the apostle, not as isolated bearers of meaning. Formulated in terms of modern linguistics, "faith" and "flesh" were ordinary words for Paul, and frequently he used them in that way, but he also used them to express very specific meanings, faith when used in relationship to God and to Christ, and flesh in the context of sin, righteousness, and the Law.

One of the characteristic features of the history of religion school's method of inquiry was to trace similar—that is, parallel—formulations of religious and popular philosophical ideas in the Hellenistic environment of the New Testament and in the New Testament itself, in an attempt to understand the language and thinking of the New Testament. In a sense, they investigated not only the meanings of individual words, as one would do for a lexicon, but also the meanings of larger formulations. They realized that in expressing their thoughts the New Testament authors did not make use only of individual terms, but also of larger thought complexes and formulations—for example, the conception of a savior who was a son of God, having been born, not of a human father and mother, but of a virgin through divine intervention (Mt 1:18-25, Lk 1:26-38), or of salvation as participation in the death and resurrection of the cult deity (cf. Gal 2:20, Rom 6:3-4). The idea was not that the New Testament authors specifically borrowed from their environment, but that they participated in the common expressions of Hellenistic antiquity, which were as much their own as they were of the religious and popular philosophical thinking of their time.

These formulations, more than single terms, but in their usage similar to single terms—macroterms one might call them—constituted the conceptual environment in which New Testament Christianity articulated its experience of salvation in Christ. The formulations were shared means of expression that also could be found in other writings of Hellenistic antiquity; the experience and understanding of salvation in Christ Jesus that were expressed by means of them were not shared. These were distinct, notwithstanding the common means of expression. Thus as the meanings of such terms as "faith" and "flesh" depended on the way in which Paul used them, so the meanings of larger shared thought complexes and formulations were also dependent on the way they were used by the New Testament authors.

At the most elementary level what Christianity expressed was that salvation was through Christ Jesus, and not through some other cult figure. But then Christ was not a hollow symbol that could be filled with any meaning, even though all New Testament writers did not share exactly the same understanding of that meaning. The understanding that salvation was through Christ gave very specific meaning to the conception of salvation in the thinking of each of these writers. It is the task of the interpreter of the New Testament to uncover that meaning as it was brought to expression in the various formulations of New Testament Christianity, which means that one has to distinguish between the message of New Testament Christianity and the formulations by means of which that message was brought to expression.

2. The distinction between the means of expression and what is expressed was aired in a different way in the controversy between Karl Barth and Rudolf Bultmann concerning *Sachkritik*, a critique based on the subject matter. In Barth's famous little commentary on 1 Corinthians, *Die Auferstehung der Toten*,[4] he insisted that in chapter 15 (which he considered the conceptual center of the letter), Paul was not talking about the "last" things that were to happen when history came to an end (apocalyptic), but the "end" that one encounters at every moment of one's existence before God (eschatology).

In his review of the commentary, Bultmann[5] affirmed Barth's interpretation wholeheartedly, and in his subsequent work formulated it as the "dehistorisizing of eschatology." However, contrary to Barth, he maintained that while speaking of the end things, Paul had available as means of expression only the language of the last things; he gave expression to his thoughts on the end things in terms of the last things. The task of interpretation was to distinguish between the means of expression and what was expressed—that is, between the expression and the subject matter. According to Bultmann, Barth interpreted the subject matter correctly, but failed to distinguish between the subject matter and its expression.

Significantly, Bultmann's position left interpretation open-ended in the sense that it preserved interest in what he interpreted here as only the means of expression, distinct from the subject matter. This openness made it possible for subsequent interpretation of the New Testament in the school of Bultmann to recognize that what Bultmann, following Barth, interpreted as mere expression was in fact part of the subject matter. In particular Ernst Käsemann reaffirmed apocalypticism as an integral part of Paul's thinking.[6]

---

[4]Karl Barth, *Die Auferstehung der Toten* (Zollikon-Zürich: Evangelischer Verlag, 1921); trans., *The Resurrection of the Dead*, by H. J. Stenning (New York: Revell, 1933).

[5]Rudolf Bultmann, "Karl Barth, Die Auferstehung der Toten," *Theologische Blätter* 5 (1925) 1-24; reprinted in Rudolf Bultmann, *Glauben und Verstehen, Gesammelte Aufsätze* (Tübingen: J.C.B. Mohr [Paul Siebeck] 1958) 1:38-64; trans., "Karl Barth, The Resurrection of the Dead," in *Faith and Understanding*, by L. P. Smith (New York: Harper and Row, 1969) 66-94.

[6]Ernst Käsemann, "Die Anfänge christlicher Theologie," *Zeitschrift für Theologie und Kirche* 57 (1960) 162-85. See also "Zum Thema der urchristlichen Apokalyptik," *Zeitschrift für Theologie und Kirche* 59 (1962) 257-84; reprinted in *Exegetische Versuche und Besinnungen* (Göttingen: Vandenhoeck und Ruprecht, 1964) 2:82-131; trans., "The Beginnings of Christian Theology," and "On the Subject of Primitive Christian Apocalyptic," by W. J. Montague, in *New Testament Questions of Today* (London: SCM Press, 1969) 82-137.

The distinction between expression and subject matter had even greater significance for Bultmann with regard to the mythological formulation of New Testament thought.[7] Against earlier attempts to deal with the problem by simply *eliminating* the myths, Bultmann insisted that they should be *interpreted* in a systematic program of demythologizing—that is, by distinguishing the New Testament proclamation from the mythological language in which it was expressed. Eliminating the myths meant to abandon the message that was expressed by means of them as well. According to Bultmann, even though the mythical language itself was no longer meaningful in the present, the message expressed by means of it remained relevant. It was the task of interpretation to allow that message to speak again, distinct from the earlier, mythical means of expressing it.

Bultmann understood mythical language to have been a roundabout way of speaking, as objectifying speech. The New Testament proclamation addressed the human subject in her or his existence before God—in the sense of Barth's "end"—but it did so indirectly, by speaking about objects, such as sin, the flesh, demons, and the world. The New Testament proclamation was a form of address, but it was formulated in such a way that it frequently seemed to be giving information about things. According to Bultmann there was a double problem with the New Testament language in contemporary interpretation: Not only was it formulated mythologically; it also spoke in a roundabout, objectifying way. In Bultmann's program of demythologizing one should thus distinguish two features: on the one hand, the necessity to reformulate the New Testament kerygma in nonmythological language, and on the other, formulating it in a way that avoids the roundabout, objectifying mode of speech of the mythological language, allowing the kerygma to be heard as a form of address.

Both of these tasks were carried out by Bultmann in the single program of demythologizing, but they should nevertheless be distinguished. It was for the second task that he made use of Martin Heidegger's existentialist language— a task, it should be remembered, that he had already recognized in the discussions with Barth concerning the interpretation of 1 Corinthians 15. But demythologizing does not have to be defined in existentialist language. Ernst Käsemann does not understand it in that way. He still insists on the necessity of demythologizing, but does not want to limit such a program to a purely ex-

---

[7]Rudolf Bultmann, "Neues Testament und Mythologie," *Kerygma und Mythos*, ed. H.-W. Bartsch (Hamburg: Herbert Reich, 1948; 2d ed., 1951) 1:15-48; trans., "The New Testament and Mythology," in *Kerygma and Myth*, by Reginald Fuller (London: SPCK, 1953) 1:1-44.

istentialist, dehistorisizing interpretation.[8] For Käsemann the world and history remain of decisive importance; eschatology cannot be dehistorisized in an existentialist interpretation in which the encounter with God does not concern what takes place on the plane of history.

It has been protested against Bultmann's program—most forcefully by Karl Jaspers[9]—that people today do not think less mythologically than in New Testament times. The statement may be correct, but not the protest. The mythological world view of New Testament times is no longer ours. The mythological concepts of the New Testament, since they are not ours, distract from the message. In debates about whether Jesus was born of a virgin, or whether he was raised physically from the dead, the meaning expressed in these formulations is moved into the background. The task of interpretation should be to attend to the message without being distracted by debates concerning the historicity or mythological nature of the means of its expression. Bultmann may have exaggerated when he insisted that people today no longer think mythologically. Yet it would certainly be naive to ignore that innumerable people today are distracted by the mythical conceptions of the New Testament.

The task of interpretation is to move beyond the expressions to what was expressed. But it has become clear that an existentialist interpretation is far too limiting to accomplish the task adequately. The limitation is not only that it does not take into account concerns about the world and history, as Käsemann correctly pointed out. The problem is in substituting one system of thought for another, philosophical/systematic-theological thinking for mythological thinking. The most important reason why Bultmann was able to take existentialist thinking so much for granted was that it was the way of thinking, the mood, of Europe between the two world wars and immediately after the second world war. In contrast, the mood of our own time has become much more social, with a concern for what is happening in history. It is no longer the individual who stands alone, but a social being who stands before God; a person involved with responsibility in history, in what happens to others.

With that observation we have already moved to what is at the heart of this essay—the polarity between salvation as a gift and as a demand; salvation as something that is granted freely by God, disregarding the degree to which one is deserving, and salvation as life in obedience to God's demand; the believer

---

[8]"Demythologizing . . . cannot be identified with existentialist interpretation, as little as it can dispense with it." *Der Ruf der Freiheit* (Tübingen: J.C.B. Mohr [Paul Siebeck], 1968) 179; trans., *Jesus Means Freedom*, by Frank Clarke (Philadelphia: Fortress Press, 1970).

[9]Karl Jaspers, "Wahrheit und Unheil der bultmannschen Entmythologisierung," *Kerygma und Mythos*, 3:9-59; reprinted in Karl Jaspers and Rudolf Bultmann, *Der Frage der Entmythologisierung* (München: R. Piper & Co. Verlag, 1964) 7-55; trans., "Myth and Religion," in *Myth and Christianity* (New York: Noonday Press, 1958) 3-56.

as an individual standing alone before God at every moment and as someone who participates responsibly in the ongoing events of history. It is the polarity of the Fourth Evangelist's "the hour is coming and now is when the dead will hear the voice of the son of God, and those who hear will live" (John 5:25) and the First Evangelist's "not everyone who says to me, 'Lord, Lord,' will enter into the kingdom of heaven, but whoever does the will of my father who is in the heavens" (Mt 7:21).

What does one do with such contrary meanings of salvation in the single New Testament canon? The difficulty becomes even more acute when both sides of the polarity are affirmed by a single author, Paul, who writes in the same letter: "Not the hearers of the Law are justified before God, but the doers of the Law will be justified" (Rom 2:13) and "Out of works of the Law no one will be justified before him . . . but now the righteousness of God has been revealed without the Law . . . for all who believe" (Rom 3:20-22). How can he affirm the validity of such contrary conceptions of justification before God, as recognition for what one has done and as a gift of God, based solely on God's kindness? In the history of New Testament interpretation attempts constantly have been made to reconcile Paul's contradictory conceptions of salvation/justification, and the contradictions in the understanding of salvation by different authors in the New Testament canon. All of them have been made at the cost of the full meaning of both conceptions, salvation by faith and salvation through obedience to God's will.

B. TOWARD A NEW METHOD OF INTERPRETATION

1. A more satisfactory solution to the problem of these contradictions may be provided by a better understanding of myth. Such an understanding was suggested by the anthropologist Claude Lévi-Strauss, who interprets mythical thought as the attempt to cope with irresolvable contradictions.[10] If we take myth in its broadest sense as the expression of religious thought in contrast with philosophical/systematic-theological thinking, and not in the narrow sense of something unhistorical, Lévi-Strauss's understanding of myth makes it possible to maintain the full meaning of both sides of the polarity, salvation as a gift and as one's due for doing the will of God. In that way demythologizing becomes unnecessary, and Bultmann's intention of uncovering the mean-

---

[10]Claude Lévi-Strauss, "The Structural Study of Myth," *Journal of American Folklore* 78 (1955) 428-444. Translated with some additions and modifications as "La Structure des mythes," *Anthropologie Structurale* (Paris: Plon, 1958) 1:225-55; trans. *Structural Anthropology*, by Claire Jacobson and Brooke Grundfest Schoeps (New York: Basic Books, 1963) 206-31.

ing behind the mythological language of the New Testament may still be achieved.

Lévi-Strauss's method of uncovering the meaning expressed in mythical texts is to read them not only syntagmatically—that is, with the flow of the stories—but also paradigmatically—that is, by tabulating the recurrence of similar story elements or what he calls mythemes. Examination of a sufficient number of mythemes enables him to discern structural patterns of oppositions between groups of them. He compares the process with reading a musical score, not only horizontally with regard to its melody, but also vertically with regard to the harmony of the various voices of the instruments or singers.

This can be illustrated in the New Testament, somewhat arbitrarily, by noting that the recurrence of those expressions that present the human being as a child of God over and against those that present human destiny as enslavement to sin. There is a parallel polarity in those "mythemes" that express an understanding of the world as God's creation over and against those that express a realization that the world is under the domination of evil. Clearly, New Testament Christianity shared these mythemes with other religions of Hellenistic antiquity and with the popular philosophy of the time, as the history of religion school had long recognized. Lévi-Strauss's structural method makes it possible to move beyond the mere establishment of parallel expressions to their roots in the human predicament of belonging to, if one could put it in that way, heaven and earth, or more radically, good and evil, or life and death. The task of interpreting an individual text would then be to see how the author copes with what appear to be these irreconcilable contradictions in human existence.

At the root of Lévi-Strauss's structural method is the insight of the Swiss linguist, Ferdinand de Saussure,[11] that meanings do not reside in words, but in the structural relationships between words. That is the insight anticipated by Wrede when he pointed out that New Testament authors did not operate with precisely defined concepts. For example, terms such as "faith" and "flesh" should be considered within the framework of their usage by Paul. Lévi-Strauss extended de Saussure's insight to formulations larger than single words—to what, in the context of the interpretation of myths, he called mythemes. He addressed the significance of this in his important review[12] of the

---

[11]*Cours de linguistique générale*, published posthumously by Charles Bally and Albert Sechehaye, with the collaboration of A. Reidlinger (Paris: Payot, 1910); trans., *Course in General Linguistics*, by Wade Baskin (New York: Philosophical Library, 1959).

[12]"La Structure et la forme. Réflexions sur un ouvrage de Vladimir Propp," in *Cahiers de l'Institut de science économique appliquée* 9 (1960) 3-36, and simultaneously under the title "L'Analyse morphologique des contes russes" in *International Journal of Slavic Linguistics and Poetics* 3 (1960); reprinted in *Anthopologie struturale deux* (Paris: Plon, 1973) 139-73; trans., "Structure and Form: Reflections on a Work by Vladimir Propp" in *Structural Anthropology* by Monique Layton (New York: Basic Books, 1976) 2:115-45.

famous work of the Russian formalist Vladimir Propp, *Morphology of the Folktale*.[13] Although Lévi-Strauss was not directly influenced by Propp's 1928 work—his first encounter with the work was in the 1958 English translation—he recognized with genuine appreciation its indirect influence through his association with Roman Jakobson. The critical edge of Lévi-Strauss's review was to point out the difference between Propp's morphology and a structural approach.

Propp's investigation had shown that fairy tales could be analyzed in terms of thirty-one functions (actions) and seven character roles. An example of such a function would be "the villain abducts a person," which could appear concretely in different tales as a dragon kidnapping the tsar's daughter, a witch kidnapping a boy, or older brothers abducting the bride of a younger brother. Not every function or every role is present in every tale, but Propp found that the sequence of those that were present remained the same. Thus, behind all the fairy tales there appears to be only one primeval tale.

Lévi-Strauss's critique pointed out that the morphologist separated form from content whereas the structuralist understood form and content to be inseparable. Propp interpreted the structure of the fairy tale as a chronological succession of story elements or functions that were qualitatively distinct, each constituting an independent "genre." Through structural study of myth it had become possible to establish that functions (Lévi-Strauss's mythemes) were not linked in a mere succession, but that many of them were transformations of one and the same function. Thus it became possible to reduce them further. So, for example, what Propp identified as two distinct functions—the combat in which the hero engages and the difficult task he performs—became recognizable as transformations of one and the same function. What made it possible to recognize such actions as transformations of the same function was the realization that they were not discrete, but functioned in relationship to others.

With regard to our own material this means that we could now move beyond the individual formulations in terms of which New Testament Christians gave expression to the experience of salvation in Christ as if they were discrete entities, to the recognition of them as transformations of functions that had meaning only in relationship to other functions, similarly transformed into concrete formulations. In this way the structure of the conceptual world in which New Testament Christians experienced salvation in Christ is exposed. Thus we have an even better understanding of their language and thinking than had been possible for the history of religion school. That school had still taken the formulations very much as individual expressions, even though anyone

---

[13]2d ed., rev. and ed. with a Preface by Louis A. Wagner (Austin: University of Texas Press, 1968).

who has read Richard Reitzenstein's *Hellenistische Mysterien-Religionen*[14] knows that the thrust of a work such as that was toward the entire conceptual world in which Christianity was born. Investigation of individual formulations was no mere "parallelomania" for the history of religion school but an attempt to understand the language and thinking of that time. For our purposes one can consider the work of Lévi-Strauss as a further step in what was started by the history of religion school.

2. One final development in the interpretation of texts deserves our attention: the very precise method for investigating the way meaning is expressed in texts undertaken by Algirdas Greimas, most recently with the collaboration of Joseph Courtés in *Sémiotique: Dictionnaire raisonné de la théorie du langage*.[15] For our purposes it is probably best to take as point of departure the generative trajectory presented by Greimas and Courtés and to comment on its various parts.

The trajectory has two components, one syntactic and the other semantic, clarifying how words and larger units are linked (syntax), and how meaning is brought to expression by such linkage in a text (semantics). The generative trajectory is not intended to reveal how a text is produced (what is called pragmatics in linguistic theory), as if an author goes through the various levels as she or he produces a text. The generative trajectory is an abstract presentation

GENERATIVE TRAJECTORY			
		syntactic component	semantic component
Semio-narrative structures	deep level	FUNDAMENTAL SYNTAX	FUNDAMENTAL SEMANTICS
	surface level	SURFACE NARRATIVE SYNTAX	NARRATIVE SEMANTICS
Discursive structures		DISCURSIVE SYNTAX Discursivization actualization temporalization spatialization	DISCURSIVE SEMANTICS Thematization Figurativization

---

[14](Stuttgart: B.G. Teubner, 1910); reprint of the 3d ed., (Darmstadt: Wissenschaftliche Buchgesellschaft, 1956); trans., *Hellenistic Mystery-Religions*, by John E. Steely, (Pittsburgh: Pickwick Press, 1978).

[15](Paris: Classiques Hachette, 1979); trans., *Semiotics and Language*, by Larry Crist, Daniel Patte, et al. (Bloomington: Indiana University Press, 1982).

of what is involved grammatically in a text. As one moves through the various levels of the trajectory it is not as if one moves from earlier to later stages in the production of the text. All the features are present at the same time. There is also no pretense that these features are concretely present, hidden in the text. They are abstractions, products of linguistic theory, by means of which it becomes possible to understand the grammar of a text, syntactically and semantically.

It is not possible within the framework of the present discussion to give attention to every aspect of this proposed grammatical schema. An important detail of the syntactic component at its surface level (the surface narrative syntax) is that Greimas further generalized or abstracted Propp's schema of thirty-one functions and seven character roles as the means of analyzing fairy tales to a schema with four phases involving two subject roles and one object by means of which any discourse can be analyzed.

NARRATIVE SCHEMA			
I Need	**II Preparedness**	**III Performance**	**IV Sanction**
A subject of a circumstance, disjoined from a desirable object, or conjoined with an undesirable object.	An active subject, willing or obliged, and able (having the power), to overcome the need, specified in I, by a performance.	The active subject performing the action transforming the circumstance specified in I into its opposite.	Recognition of the success or failure of the performance, or of the achievement of a desired value.

3. How this schema functions in the analysis of a text can be illustrated by a presentation of the results of an analysis of Romans 4:18-22. The actual analysis cannot be presented here because that in itself would take up the space of a short article.

The passage ends with the statement, "therefore it was counted as righteousness for him" (4:22). Hoping against hope, Abraham believed God's promise that he would be the father of many nations (4:18); that faith was counted as righteousness for him. The problem with statements such as these is that they seem to take faith as a work for which one, in this case Abraham, receives a reward. But we know that, according to Paul, faith is the very contrary of a work; justification by faith is to receive from God an undeserved gift because of his kindness. That can be presented readily by means of the schema.

God promised Abraham that he would have many descendants after both he and Sarah were no longer capable of having a child. As the intended active subject, the pair, Abraham and Sarah, were no longer capable (phase II) of performing the action of having a child (phase III) that would satisfy their need (phase I) of having one. God himself did not carry out the performance of transforming their lack of a child into having one; what God in effect told Abraham was that he would *enable* them to have a child even though they were both already beyond the age of childbearing. God's action (phase III) of transforming their lack of ability to have a child into the ability to do so is a subprogram of phase II of the main program, the program in which Abraham and Sarah were to act together as the active subject to bring to life the promised child. God acts in a subprogram of phase II of the main program to enable Abraham and Sarah to perform the required performance of that program. It is this subprogram that Abraham sanctions with his faith—hoping against hope, he believed that God was capable of what he promised (cf. esp. 4:21). Faith, therefore, is not a work, but the sanctioning of God's work. When it concerns Christ, it is the sanctioning of God's work in Christ.

But what then happens when Abraham's faith is sanctioned by God, who counts it as righteousness for him? Does that not mean that Abraham is an active subject, one who works, and that he is rewarded with justification for his faith? This is indeed the case, but it is once more in a subprogram, in this case of phase IV of the main program, his sanctioning of God's ability to enable him and Sarah to have a child. Faith is thus indeed a performance in which the believer is engaged, but in a subprogram, not a main program. In a main program it is an act of sanctioning God's ability to do what he promised in the present text, or typically in the New Testament of what God has done in Christ for the believer. In this way it becomes possible to see how faith is an action in which the believer engages, but not a work for which the believer receives a reward, because in its fundamental sense it is a sanction of God's action and only in a derived sense is it in itself an action.

It is possible to analyze these statements even further syntactically. One may move to an even more abstract or deeper level by using only symbols for active subjects, subjects of circumstance, objects, actions, and placing all of these on semiotic squares, showing how a series of statements are linked syntactically. The above discussion already touched on such a linkage by showing how God's promise to Abraham is related to Abraham's faith being counted for him as righteousness.

Thus one can analyze the promise that Abraham and Sarah would have a child as follows. First Abraham and Sarah having a child.

$$F_1[S_1 => (S_1 \cup O_1) => (S_1 \cap O_1)]$$

This diagram F_1 represents a single narrative program or function, (the action through which Abraham and Sarah come to have a child); the brackets delimit the extent of the function; S_1 the active subject (Abraham and Sarah who together overcome their lack of having a child); $=>$ the action of the active subject which is to transform one circumstance into another. The two sets of parentheses represent two circumstances, first of the subject of circumstance (in this case also Abraham and Sarah) disjoined from an object, O_1 (the child), which is then transformed into its opposite, the subject of circumstance conjoined with the object (Abraham and Sarah having a child), $\cup$ represents disjunction, $>$ the transformation from one circumstance to its opposite, and $\cap$ conjunction.

If one wants to take Abraham and Sarah getting a child more specifically in the sense of Sarah giving birth to it, the function would be written.

$$F_2[S_2 => (S_1 \cup O_1) => (S_1 \cap O_1)]$$

In this diagram Sarah, represented by S_2, is the active subject who transforms her and Abraham's circumstance of being disjoined from the object—being without a child—into the opposite circumstance of being conjoined with it.

According to our text Abraham and Sarah were no longer able to have children, but when God promised Abraham that he would become the father of many nations, Abraham knew that against all expectations God would make it possible for them to have a child.

$$F_3[S_3 => (S_1 \cup O_2) => (S_1 \cap O_2)]$$

In this diagram S_3 represents God, and O_2 the ability to have children.

The analysis shows clearly what we already know, that God does not actually just give Abraham and Sarah a child—as, for example, by calling one forth from a rock (cf. Mt 3:9). God is not the active subject who transforms Abraham and Sarah's childlessness into having a child; he *enables* them to have their own child when they no longer have the ability.

We can now present the narrative programs F_1 and F_3 in their relatedness on a semiotic square:

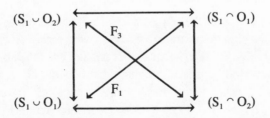

The semiotic square is based on the logical square. A logical square shows what all the logical possibilities are, whereas a semiotic square shows which of these are actually the case, and how an existing case is changed into its opposite according to the rules of logic. (Actually Greimas interprets the semiotic square slightly differently as a modification of the logical square.[16] However, since all our thinking should take place according to the rules of logic it is advantageous to keep the functioning of the semiotic square in conformity with the logical square.) Most readers will remember how the logical square functions. The two top corners represent contraries—both of them cannot be true at the same time—and the two bottom corners subcontraries—both of which can be true at the same time. The relationship between the top right and the bottom left and between the bottom right and the top left is a contradiction—that is, the one is the direct contradiction of the other. The relationship between each contrary pole to the subcontrary pole below it is implication—that is, if the top right corner is the case the bottom right corner also has to the base, but not the inverse; the bottom right corner can be the case even if the top right corner is not. The same applies to the left side of the square. This can be shown clearly by placing the four circumstances of our semiotic square on a logical square.

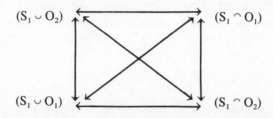

$$(S_1 \cup O_2)$$ .... $$(S_1 \cap O_1)$$

$$(S_1 \cup O_1)$$ .... $$(S_1 \cap O_2)$$

If Abraham and Sarah do not have the ability to have a child $(S_1 \cup O_2)$ it implies that they also do not have a child $(S_1 \cup O_1)$, and if they have a child $(S_1 \cap O_1)$ it implies that they also have the ability to have one $(S_1 \cap O_2)$. The inverse does not apply: If they do not have a child $(S_1 \cup O_1)$, that does not imply that they do not have the ability to have one $(S_1 \cup O_2)$; they could have decided not to have one. Similarly, if they have the ability to have a child $(S_1 \cap O_2)$ that does not imply that they have one $(S_1 \cap O_1)$; again, they could have decided not to have it.

If we now go back to the semiotic square, it shows the actual situation of our text and what changes or transformations were made. Abraham and Sarah did not have a child $(S_1 \cup O_1)$ because they did not have the ability to have one $(S_1 \cup O_2)$. When God promised Abraham that he would become the father of many nations, he assured him that he and Sarah would have a child, transforming $(S_1 \cup O_1)$ into $(S_1 \cap O_1)$ by the narrative program F_1. Abraham was aware that he and Sarah were both already beyond the age of childbirth $(S_1 \cup O_2)$, but he believed, hoping against hope, that God was able to do what he

[16]See the entry "Carré sémiotique," English "Square, Semiotic."

promised—that God would make it possible for them to have a child, transforming $(S_1 \cup O_2)$ into $(S_1 \cap O_2)$ by the narrative program F_3.

It is of course not necessary to analyze every statement in a story in this way, but as with the reading of a text in a foreign language—sometimes even in one's own language—it frequently becomes necessary to clarify the grammar in order to understand properly what is intended in the text. And sometimes one thinks that one understands a text precisely, until one analyzes it grammatically, only to discover that one misread it at certain points.

The discursive syntax concerns the way in which the abstract subjects and objects (presented by means of the symbols S and O in our analysis) become real, concrete characters and recognizable things in space and time in the processes of actualization, temporalization and spatialization. These are not factors in the actual production of the text, as if Paul had first thought of abstract subjects and objects and only subsequently transformed them into concrete characters in time and space. All of this is present in the text at the same time; the analysis merely abstracts from the text these features as grammatical factors in it.

4. If we now turn to the semantic component of the generative trajectory we can move from the concrete, surface level of a text, from the figures, to the deeper, more abstract levels of the narrative and fundamental semantics. At the concrete level of an actual text its meaning is expressed in figures—that is, in discourse or story elements larger than single words, the narrative programs of our syntactic analysis. They are the equivalent of Propp's and Lévi-Strauss's functions, what Lévi-Strauss also calls mythemes.

We may begin with our previous statement: "Therefore (Abraham's faith) was counted for him as righteousness" (Rom 4:22). Previously we looked at it syntactically, the way it was connected to other statements around it—in this case, preceding it. In Lévi-Strauss's sense we read it horizontally. What we need to do now is to read the statement paradigmatically as well—that is, vertically—by looking at other occurrences of the same statement in Paul. One may employ different strategies in going about this. For example, one could look for every statement in which righteousness and every statement in which faith occurs. One would try to see how such series of statements line up as transformations of the same functions or narrative programs, expressing a single theme. As an example, I produce several statements from the first part of Romans.

> Not the hearers of the Law are righteous before God, but the doers will be found righteous (2:13).
> Therefore, from works of the Law, nobody will be found righteous before him (3:20).
> Without the law, the righteousness of God has been revealed . . . through the faith of Christ Jesus for all who believe (3:21-22).

Do we destroy the Law by faith? By no means! We establish the Law (3:31).

If Abraham was found righteous because of works, he would have [reason for] pride, but not before God (4:2).

Abraham believed and it was counted as righteousness for him (4:3)

To the person who does not work, but believes in him who counts the ungodly righteous, her/his faith is counted for her/him as righteousness (4:4).

David pronounces blessings on the person whom God counts righteous without works (4:6).

For Abraham faith was counted as righteousness (4:10).

He received the sign of circumcision, the seal of the faith, while uncircumcized, that he would be the father of all who believe through uncircumcision, [and] that it would also be counted for them as righteousness (4:11).

[He would be] the father of the circumcized for those who are not only of the circumcized, but who follow in the footsteps of the faith, while uncircumcized, of our father Abraham (4:12).

For a thorough interpretation of Paul every statement he makes on topics such as these should be taken into consideration. Our consideration of these statements can serve only as an example. Nevertheless, they already make it possible to establish two configurations or series of figures.

a) Those who only hear the Law are not found righteous before God (2:13).

Those who do what the Law requires will be found righteous (2:13).

[Because of their disobedience, (cf. 3:10-19)] nobody will be found righteous before God on the basis of works of the Law (3:20).

If Abraham was found righteous because of works, he would have had reason for pride (4:2).

To these we can add:

The reward for the person who works is not calculated as a kindness, but in accordance with what is done (4:4).

b) The righteousness of God has been revealed without the law . . . through the faith of Christ Jesus for all who believe (3:21-22).

Abraham believed and it was counted as righteousness for him (4:3).

To the person who does not work, but believes in him who counts the ungodly righteous, her/his faith is counted for her/him as righteousness (4:4).

David pronounces blessings on the person whom God counts righteous without works (4:6).

Faith was counted for Abraham as righteousness (4:10).

Abraham received the sign of circumcision, the seal of the faith, while uncircumcized, that he would be the father of all who believe through uncircumcision [and] that it would also be counted for them as righteousness (4:11).

Abraham was to be the father of the circumcized for those who were not only of the circumcized, but who also followed in the footsteps of his faith, while uncircumcized (4:12).

The two series of figures give expression to two themes: a) that the basis of justification is one's deeds and b) that the basis of justification is one's faith in God. These are, of course, the most general themes; one could also identify subthemes, differentiating between more specific groups of figures, but our concern here is to move to the most general or most abstract features of the Pauline texts.

The two themes stand over and against each other as opposed ways of finding justification. If we now move to the deeper level of the values to which these themes give expression, we know, as one of the probably most well-known facts about Paul, that for him only justification through faith, not through works of the Law, had salvific value. Whatever value justification by works may have had, it was not salvation. Thus one might conclude that when he wrote that there was a justification for doing what was required by the Law as the formulation of God's will, he understood that kind of justification to have had a value different from salvation; namely, it gave reason to be proud of one's achievements. With that it becomes clear that the issue in the interpretation of Paul in this regard is not whether or not justification is also possible on the basis of works. Paul says both—in one instance that it can be (Rom 2:13) and in another that it cannot be by any means (Rom 3:20). One has to consider how he uses the term "justification" in each case. We are reminded of Wrede's comment that Paul is not systematic in his usage of terms; that one has to ask in each case in what framework he uses terms like "faith" and "flesh"; here we can add "justification." The difference between the usage of "justified" in Romans 2:13 and 3:20 may be found in its expression of different values in the two instances.

A clue to the difference may be found in Romans 4:2 where Paul qualifies his statement that if Abraham had been justified because of works he would have had reason to be proud with the phrase "but not before God." Justification on the basis of one's works gives reason to be proud, but not before God; it has value in the pride of achievement, similar to the value of possessing a prestigious automobile or diamonds, but it does not ensure the value, salvation. In Paul's sense it does not sustain one when one stands "before God," and in the interpretation of Barth, it has no value with regard to the end which one encounters at every moment when one stands before God. Access to the value, salvation, is not provided by one's own achievements; it is available only as a gift of God. Thus, according to Paul, Abraham knew, in the face of the zero of his own ability and that of his wife Sarah, that he could put his trust only in God's promise.

A careful reading of Romans 2:13 suggests that the phrase "before God" in the first part of Paul's statement, "not the hearers of the Law are just before God," is implied also in the second part, "but the doers will be justified." That would probably be the usual way in which one would read the statement. One does note, however, a certain reservation on Paul's part with regard to the symmetry of the two parts of the statement: "Not the hearers of the Law are just before God, but the doers *will be* justified." Paul himself was probably aware that the parallelism in the statement implied that "before God" also applied to the second part, but he let it go at that, except possibly for the attempt to qualify the symmetry. However, it is significant that when he uses the figure again in Romans 4:2, he explicitly adds "but not before God."

Thus it appears that in Paul the two series of figures concerning justification give expression to two very different values, salvation and pride. He evidently affirms both values. What is at the root of his protest against justification through works of the Law is that it is taken as an expression of the value of salvation. We cannot investigate the reasons for his protest here, except to mention at least one that is very explicit. Paul writes in Romans 4:14-16, "For if those who were from the Law were inheritors, faith would be empty, and the promises destroyed. For the Law creates wrath—where there is no Law there is no transgression. For that reason it is through faith, in order to be in accordance with kindness, so that the promises would be secure" (Rom 4:16). Paul knew that even if one did everything that was required by the Law, it still did not provide security, because the demand of the Law continued to press upon one. That explains the existential agony of Romans 7, which even Bultmann tried to explain away as a reference to Paul's previous existence under the Law. It also explains why he could say that he considered his own perfection under the Law as a loss (the contrary of a reward!) for the sake of what is offered in Christ (Phil 3:7-11), even though he valued works because they gave reason for pride, for self-esteem.

And yet Paul could not dispense with doing good as irrelevant for salvation, even though he never gave up his conviction that justification by faith and by works were contraries. Again and again he gets caught up in the question, if it is by faith that we are saved, why should we still strive for what is good (cf. esp. Rom 6). Notwithstanding his conviction that salvation could be found only through faith in what God offered in Christ, and not on the basis of one's own actions, Paul was unable to believe that a person who did not do what was good, but what was evil, was saved. "We who have died to sin, how can we still live in it" (Rom 6:2). That was the fundamental contradiction that Paul could not resolve, that salvation was by faith alone without works, and yet, not to live in accordance with what the Law required, not doing good and not

avoiding evil, contradicted being saved. Notwithstanding Martin Luther's succinct formula, *simul justus et peccator*, Paul knew that no one could live as a
sinner, that as sinners we were not saved. To put it very sharply, Paul knew that
one could not live by God's kindness alone, one lived by also doing the will
of God. Thus it is not surprising that his letters are replete with admonitions.

Paul himself was not altogether unaware of the difficulty. Twice, when he
brought the contrast between the Law and faith to a pitch, he found it necessary to reaffirm their solidarity: "Is the Law then against the promises?" he
asks in Galatians 3:21, only to deny it emphatically, adding, "for if a Law with
a power to make alive had been given, justification would indeed have been
through the Law." And in Romans 2:31 he asks the inverse question: "Do we
then destroy the Law through faith? By no means! We confirm it."

We can find the reasons for Paul's difficulties if we move our analysis a
step further, to the fundamental semantics, to the microuniverse of the text.
Greimas and Courtés distinguish two microuniverses, the one individual,
which finds expression in the polarity life/death, and the other collective or
social, which finds its expression in the polarity culture/nature.[17] The polarity
culture/nature may not be sufficiently abstract, and thus also not universal. It
may be better to identify it tentatively as order/chaos.

In these two microuniverses we can recognize the distinction Barth made
between end things and last things, between what Bultmann called eschatology and history, between the human being as an individual who stands exis-
tentially alone in the face of the ultimate, and as a social being who depends
on others to find meaning in her or his existence. The two are irreconcilable.
To put it in terms of Paul's thinking, it is not possible to depend solely on
God's kindness and at the same time make an appeal in terms of one's achievements. Paul knew that very well when he stated that pride was excluded not by
the principle of works but by the principle of faith (Rom 3:27), that the reward
for a person's achievements was not calculated as a kindness, but in accordance with what was due (4:4). But it was precisely in such a context that he
felt the necessity of reaffirming the solidarity of works and faith: We confirm
the Law with faith (3:31).

At the roots of Paul's thinking was an insistence on the solidarity of both
principles without allowing either to be weakened by its relationship to the
other. In his microuniverse the existential and social polarities, life/death and
order/chaos, stood in irreconcilable opposition to each other, and yet he remained convinced that neither could negate the other. God's kindness stood
in irreconcilable opposition to the opposition between order and chaos, rep-

---

[17]See the entries "Micro-univers" and "Sémantique fondamentale," English "Micro-uni-
verse" and "Semantics, Fundamental."

resented in Paul's thinking by the opposition between good and evil, and yet God's kindness could not negate that distinction. Not even God could avoid punishing evil and rewarding good. There will be a day of judgment when God will judge the deeds of all mankind (cf. Rom 2:12-16). On the other hand he was equally convinced that on the basis of works no one could be justified before God; justification—that is, salvation—was possible only through faith in Christ Jesus (Gal 2:16, cf. Rom 3:20).

We can present the opposition between these two sets of polarities in Paul in a diagram.

Good ⟵――――――――――――――――――――――――――⟶ Evil

The vertical polarity can meet the horizontal at any point because what happens on the horizontal, social plane of good and evil is completely irrelevant for what happens on the vertical, existential plane of life and death; God's kindness did not depend in any way on the moral qualities of the human beneficiary. Similarly, according to Paul, what happens on the vertical, existential plane is irrelevant for what happens on the horizontal; the reward for the person who works is not given as a kindness, but in accordance with what is due (Rom 4:4). Anything less would be to compromise both. The contradiction in his thought, the way he experienced salvation in Christ, was such that he was nevertheless also unable to accept that the two polarities were irrelevant for each other.

This schema now also makes it possible to clarify the difference between Matthew and John in their conceptions of salvation, between Matthew's, "No one who calls me, 'Lord, Lord,' will enter into the kingdom of heaven, but the person who does the will of my father who is in heaven" (7:21), and John's, "The hour is coming, and now is, when the dead will hear the voice of the Son of God, and those who hear will live" (5:25). In Matthew's understanding the vertical dimension is collapsed into the horizontal.

Good
= Life ⟵――――――――――――――――――――――――――⟶ Evil
                                                        = Death

In direct contradiction of Paul's conviction that salvation was only through faith in Christ Jesus, and could not be based on what one does in obedience to the Law, Matthew here and elsewhere insists that any appeal to Christ would be useless, because what ultimately mattered was one's deeds. This understanding finds its most powerful expression in Matthew's description of the last judgment where persons are judged without mercy on the basis of deeds they did or failed to do without realizing that their salvation depended on it (Mt 25:31-46).

John's position is the exact opposite. In his understanding the horizontal polarity is absorbed into the vertical.

$$\uparrow \quad \begin{array}{l} \text{Life} \\ = \text{Solidarity} \\ \\ \text{Alienation} \\ = \text{Death} \end{array}$$

This view is expressed, for example, in chapter 4, where the alienation between Jews and Samaritans is overcome not as social reconciliation but as the absorption of the Samaritan villagers into the community of true believers who worship the Father in spirit and truth, when they recognize Jesus as the savior of the world.

It appears thus that the contradiction between faith and works is at the root of New Testament thought. The contradiction remains unresolved in Paul's thought, whereas in Matthew and in John a fundamental choice has been made, resolving it in one way or the other. Nevertheless, they all belong to the single canon of the New Testament, and so what is resolved in Matthew and in John individually remains unresolved in the canon to which both of them belong. This would be a serious problem for a collection of documents from which one expects systematic unity. In a collection of religious writings, however, what appears systematically as a weakness could be a sign of richness. However, then the New Testament canon should not be taken as a rule of faith, in the sense of a doctrine, but as a religious framework within which the Christian is called upon to understand herself or himself.

In that sense, any attempt to resolve the contradiction between salvation as a gift and as a demand, to use Frank Stagg's terms, would be to reduce that framework for the sake of a single systematic principle. In a sense that is what we have in Matthew and in John when each is taken alone. The presence of both of them in the canon is what gives the New Testament its specific character as a collection of writings that affirms that salvation can only be received as a gift that frees the recipient from dependence on the things of the world (John 5:25), *and* that it can be found only in active obedience to the call to engage in what is happening in the world (Mt 7:21, cf. 25:31-46). In that regard Paul is the most religious of them all, and one can probably also say the most profound, because of his inability to resolve the contradiction, and his refusal to compromise on either side of it.

THE NEW TESTAMENT AND ETHICS: HOW DO WE GET FROM THERE TO HERE?

ROBIN SCROGGS
CHICAGO THEOLOGICAL SEMINARY
CHICAGO, ILLINOIS 60637

To write an essay on this topic to honor Frank Stagg is at the same time an honor for me. The comprehensive study *Woman in the World of Jesus* is full of ethical implications for evaluating Scripture and for helping to influence our own ecclesiastical posture toward male and female in the twentieth century. What I attempt here is, however, full of dangers and perhaps even foolhardiness! In these pages I wish to ask what is actually a timeworn question: How can the NT be used to inform ethical discussions in our world today? Unfortunately, I do not think this question has received a definitive answer even among the most conservative theologians and scholars. Nor am I so naive as to think this essay can provide such an answer. Perhaps, at least, I can raise the question again, to see what proposals have been made recently.

And here I ask the question both of scholars of the NT and of ethics, for it seems to me that there has not been sufficient dialogue between the two disciplines. How do these different disciplines see the issue and how might they mutually inform each other? What can the specialist in ethics learn from the biblical scholars? Perhaps even more crucially, how can the biblical scholar profit from methodological discussions of the ethicist? As James Gustafson has complained: "Those who are specialists in ethics generally lack the intensive and proper training in biblical studies, and those who are specialists in biblical studies often lack sophistication in ethical thought."[1] I can only hope that the potential fruitfulness of crossing fields of study may outweigh the dangers in this essay of oversimplifying the achievements of both disciplines.

Let me first state the problem as simply as I can and then review representative approaches from the two disciplines—although it will be obvious that the whole discussion does not deal with conservative perspectives. As one embedded in "mainline" or "liberal" tradition, I must leave reflection about conservative scholarship to those more knowledgeable than I am.

We are all acquainted with various forms of the old story about a lost driver from the city who stops to ask directions to a town from an aged rural native. "Well," the driver is told, "It's over that-a-way, but you can't get there from here." That is the problem in a nutshell. How do you get from here to there, or there to here, depending upon your starting point? Or can we? In what ways is it legitimate to use ethical pronouncements in the NT to inform decision making about present ethical problems? This is not in itself an exegetical problem—hence this essay will not deal with substantive issues. The problem can be labeled theological, hermeneutical, or methodological, and all of the kinds of thinking pointed to by these terms play a role in attempting to get from there to here.

If anything simple can be said about this issue, it is that the matter is complex. Even those who claim to operate out of simple solutions find, on careful analysis, that the issue is more difficult than they might at first have thought. For the theologian, at one extreme, who would claim that the Bible is the eternal, infallible word of God and thus that the moral injunctions of the NT can be instantly applied to today's problems, the way is not easy. To take but one obvious example, which NT evaluation is to be applied to the issue of male/female—equality or subordination of female to male?[2] At the other extreme, how would those theologians who declare the biblical statements obsolete judgments of an outmoded culture claim the decisions they do make to be Christian?

Assuming that most of us stand somewhere between these two extremes, the way from there to here is perhaps even more fraught with peril. If the NT positions are varied, perhaps even at times contradictory, if judgment about contemporary problems depends on which ethical philosophy is deemed correct, how does one fit the various pieces together to form a coherent and con-

---

[1]J. Gustafson, "The Place of Scripture in Christian Ethics: A Methodological Study," now in his collection of essays, *Theology and Christian Ethics* (Philadelphia: Pilgrim Press, 1974) 121.

[2]Fuller theologian Paul Jewett in his book (*Man as Male and Female* [Grand Rapids: Eerdmans, 1975]) has well demonstrated the complexity of this issue and has shown that hermeneutically no simple application of "The Bible" to contemporary problems is possible.

vincing whole? Do "deontology" or "consequentialist" mean anything to the biblical scholar? Does "eschatology" mean anything to the ethicist?

INTERPRETATIONS BY CHRISTIAN ETHICISTS

James Gustafson. In 1970 Gustafson published a seminal essay, "The Place of Scripture in Christian Ethics; a Methodological Study," a comprehensive yet succinct statement that one ethicist has called "the finest analysis of Scripture and ethics that I know."[3] Gustafson discussed four different ways Scripture can be appropriated by those who take it seriously as a medium of revealed morality.

1. Judgment is made about a contemporary situation on the basis of specific commands in Scripture. The oughts and ought nots spoken in the Bible are decisive norms by which any contemporary action is to be judged right or wrong. While this would seem to be a clear and simple hermeneutic, it has its own difficulties and uncertainties. As Gustafson wryly comments, "Even Fundamentalists have highly selective ways of using biblical evidence."[4]

2. Judgment is made on the basis of moral *ideals* found in Scripture. By "ideals" Gustafson points not only to the content of ideas—such as love and peace—but also to the historical nonrealization of such ideas. They are ideals in the sense of vision. It is here that the issue of eschatology is raised, since in the Judeo-Christian tradition the vision for the future is an eschatological vision. As we shall see below, the eschatological qualification of ethics is a troubling and decisive point for many thinkers struggling with biblical appropriation of ethics for today. If ethical ideals are accorded only a realization for the future, is it realistic or theoretically appropriate to apply them to a preeschatological historical situation? Despite, however, his introduction of such problems at this point, Gustafson does not allow eschatology to become dominant in his discussion, a factor that distinguishes him from the other thinkers to be discussed.

3. Judgment is based on the analogy between the situation in which the biblical pronouncement is made and the contemporary situation that is addressed. "Those actions of persons and groups are to be judged morally wrong

---

[3]Gustafson's essay cited in note 1 first appeared in *Interpretation* 24 (1970) 430-55. The assessment quoted is from James F. Childress, "Scripture and Christian Ethics," *Interpretation* 34 (1980) 378. Gustafson applies his approach to the issue of the U.S. invasion of Cambodia, a topic not to be resurrected in our concerns here.

[4]Gustafson, *Theology*, 131.

which are similar to actions that are judged to be wrong or against God's will under similar circumstances in scripture."[5]

Martin Hengel provides an illustration at this point.[6] He has argued forcefully that Jesus took a position of pacifism, in contrast to the Zealots and in the face of the serious oppression óf the Jewish populace in Palestine. Hengel analyzes the contemporary situation of repression in Central and South America and finds a legitimate analogy with Jesus' day. Hence Christians need to take with utmost seriousness Jesus' stance. The problem here, as Gustafson notes, is that of setting up an accurate analogy and of determining which biblical situation, rather than some other, is to be used.

4. In this posture judgment is complicated and "looser," to use Gustafson's term.[7] Scripture is seen as witnessing to a variety of positions and evaluations, while nonscriptural views and situations are also potentially relevant. Appeal *cannot* be made to one book or one text as if it spoke for all of Scripture. On the other hand, appeal *can* be made to other sources that might shed light—perhaps even better light than Scripture—on the contemporary issue addressed. As the author summarizes, "Scripture is one of the informing sources for moral judgments, but it is not sufficient in itself to make any particular judgment authoritative."[8]

Gustafson himself chooses a middle position, one closest to number 4 above.[9] He excludes the extremes of verbal inspiration and total irrelevancy. Somewhere in-between today's believer must take a stand. There is thus a dialogue between scriptural understandings, however they are defined, and the contemporary believer and the tools available in today's world.

Thomas W. Ogletree. A second example of an ethicist wrestling with scriptural realities is the recent and important book by Ogletree, *The Use of the Bible in Christian Ethics.*[10] This theologian approaches the issue in significantly different ways than does Gustafson, but they are not necessarily in conflict. Ogletree begins by outlining three ethical positions he considers important for contemporary reflection of ethical decisions.[11]

1. The *consequentialist.* This theory involves a utilitarian analysis of the *results* of actions. What is the *intentional* aim of the action and what are the

---

[5]Ibid., 133.

[6]Cf. M. Hengel, *Victory over Violence* (Philadelphia: Fortress, 1973) and my introduction to Hengel's thought in this book, xxi-xxiv.

[7]Gustafson, *Theology*, 134.

[8]Ibid.

[9]Ibid., 144-45.

[10](Philadelphia: Fortress, 1983).

[11]Ibid., 18-34.

actual results of the action chosen? The actor should decide what would be the best action to gain a desired goal; he then decides to act so that the result will obtain. That action is thus morally defensible. This means the actor must anticipate the future and the action chosen is designed to bring about that future. This future is not to be confused, however, with an eschatological future.

2. The *deontological*. The deontological position does not look ahead to consequences as much as it looks about to personal interrelatedness in the present. It asks, what *ought* I to do to exercise my correct and obligatory relations with others involved? This can lead to a rules ethic of responsibility.

3. The *perfectionist*. This perspective focuses attention on the moral development of the person. It concerns actions as means of developing and forming the personal moral agent. "A good person brings forth good deeds" could be the motto. As Ogletree comments, it aims at the "fullest realization of virtue by concrete human persons."[12]

Ogletree believes that there are strengths and weaknesses in each of these positions, but to list his evaluations is not possible here. He does claim, however, that a further perspective is necessary, no matter which theory one believes best, and he names this *historical contextualism*.[13] No society or community acts independently of its historical context. Even ethical theories are influenced by the society out of which they emerge and thus participate in the finitude of all historical reality. "We never take up our ethical inquiries in a purely rational form."[14] Both values and actions are so interwoven into the fabric of the concrete time in which agents live that it raises the question about *any* generalization of ethical statements.

In fact, an extreme view of historical contextualism might seem to militate against the appropriation of ethical values from one culture to another—the greater the separation of cultures, the less likelihood of a possible bridging. Ogletree does not appear to go so far, perhaps because he argues that historical contextualism does raise a universal question, that of the meaning of being. Yet given what the author has said about the finiteness of all cultural artifacts, it is clear that in his view no particular culture could give a universal and eternally valid answer to such a question. It may be for this reason that Ogletree stresses the raising of the question rather than the conclusiveness of the answer. Every culture *must* raise the question, and it will offer the answer out of its own finitude. Yet the answer, however finite, is vital to the construction of

---

[12]Ibid., 32.

[13]Ibid., 34-41.

[14]Ibid., 35.

ethics. "Only if we can discover some final meaning to human life are we likely to gain clear confirmation for peculiarly moral meanings."[15]

On the surface it might seem that Ogletree at this point is caught in a dilemma, if not self-contradiction. He is emphatic in his conclusion: "Temporality brings to the fore with special acuteness the question of the meaning of being."[16] I take it that he refers to a thinker's ability to look at transcultural understandings and to become painfully aware, perhaps, that different cultures give different answers to the question of being. But given the truth in historical contextualism, how can there be confidence that there is any transcultural *reality* to human existence and its meaning? To put the issue as sharply as possible: Is "the question of the meaning of being" a meaningful question?

There seems something of a hidden agenda here, and I think it comes to light in Ogletree's statement, "Thus, *though there is a structure to moral understanding which is derived from constitutive features of the human way of being in the world*, that structure always appears concretely in forms and modes which are relative to a given history with its unique experiences and its distinctive cultural legacy."[17] Almost in passing, the author affirms that there is a transcultural *reality* of the human self, however finite any specific *understanding* of the reality may be.

I dwell on this issue because it seems to me absolutely crucial in the enterprise of the use of one cultural ethical insight to inform that of another. Only if there are "constitutive features of the human way of being in the world" can one embark on the task of the possible appropriation of biblical ethics for the twentieth century world. I suspect that such an affirmation by Ogletree is not today shared by all people; it rests on an underlying theological and/or philosophical presupposition not explicitly present in Ogletree's discussion. It is probably shared, however precariously, by those concerned with the task discussed here. In Christian theology this presupposition may appear under the rubric of a doctrine of creation. Since among critical scholars and theologians today this doctrine has been radically demythologized, its status is, I suspect, more questionable than such thinkers often admit.[18] To explore the issue would take us beyond the limits of this essay. We do need to keep in mind, however, that some such presupposition lies underneath the entire discussion.

---

[15]Ibid., 38.

[16]Ibid., 40.

[17]Ibid., 36; italics added.

[18]For such a demythologized interpretation of the doctrine of creation, cf. R. Bultmann, *Primitive Christianity in its Contemporary Setting* (Cleveland: World, 1956) 15-22.

Ogletree has thus laid out his proposed scheme of contemporary ethical theory. There are consequentialist, deontological, and perfectionist postures, each of which is qualified by the finitude of the contexts out of which ethical actions are understood. But how does he apply these theories to biblical ethics? The author answers by describing certain significant strands or moments in biblical times and, where possible, identifying the ethical positions with the theories he has just described.[19]

Pentateuchal and early prophetic ethics are basically deontological. They deal with oughts and duties of persons in relation to the larger society. But already Ogletree introduces the theme of eschatology, which will concern him far more than it does Gustafson. The prophets developed a sense of two worlds, the present evil order and the new future envisioned and empowered by God. More clearly than does Gustafson, Ogletree treats such visions not primarily in terms of ideals but rather in terms of a future which it is hoped God will realize. Thus a dual world is created in which these worlds "interpenetrate each other and pull at each other, setting up a complex field of forces in tension as the concrete matrix of moral and religious existence."[20] Referring to later Jewish apocalyptic he epitomizes that view: "We must endure in the present evil age; but our hope is in the totally different age of God's triumphant glory."[21]

That this is a crucial point in Ogletree's outline can be seen in three implications, if I interpret him correctly. 1) Eschatology is lifted into prominence in a way not expected by the author's previous theoretical discussions of contemporary ethics. Eschatology in fact *confronts* ethical theory with a challenge of great importance. 2) He transforms visions of ideals (utopia) into hope in God's power (eschatology). 3) He shows that eschatology qualifies ethical action in ways that are independent of the actualization of the eschaton in the time of the actors, while at the same time showing that each action is decisively informed by that hope for the future.

Thus while he proceeds to characterize other biblical ethics in terms of his theoretical categories, his main thrust, or so it seems to me, is to use the eschatological posture to determine what is distinctive. For example, the ethics of Mark is deontological and perfectionist but is most decisively determined by awareness that the new age has already dawned.[22] "Thus, laws and commandments function not simply as statements about what we are to do, but

---

[19]Ogletree, *Use of the Bible*, 47-173.

[20]Ibid., 70-71.

[21]Ibid., 71.

[22]Here I cannot resist entering a demurrer to Ogletree's interpretation of Mark. I see little if any emphasis upon the presence of the kingdom at the redactional level of this gospel.

predominantly as specifications of who we are to become."[23] Ogletree sees eschatology as the basis for the perfectionist emphasis. Discipleship is, in fact, eschatological existence. Here is a fourth crucial dimension of the eschatological qualification of ethics which can add to the three previously mentioned: *Insofar as the community sees the eschatological future as emerging into present reality, ethics becomes not simply visionary, not simply hope; it becomes a possibility for existence in the here and now.*

This interpretation is then climaxed by Ogletree's treatment of Paul. For the Apostle, the new age is dawning in the midst of the old. The indicative takes its place along with the imperative. And the community, in which the indicative is realized, becomes different from all other social institutions. Paul's ethic is then perfectionist but only in the context of the present possibility of true obedience and the church as the eschatological community.

Ogletree's final chapter may take us beyond the confines of this essay, but the implications are so important that they deserve mention here.[24] He argues that the Pauline "now but not yet" and the "indicative/imperative" tensions are normative for the church. He thinks a dialectic eschatology (that of a Paul) to be constitutive of the church in preference to an eschatology that is purely focused on the future. A sense that the kingdom is here in power (however hidden) leads to this dialectic ethic, which in turn creates a dialectic of church over against world, in which a decisive break is made with establishment society. Such a church should manifest 1) "some degree of alienation" from the outside world and 2) "a deep involvement with a community."[25]

Whenever the church does not manifest such characteristics, it has failed its call both to its nature and its actions. Ethics and eschatology are thus not antagonistic; they are compatible, even essential to each other. In Ogletree's view, therefore, true biblical ethics is not an unrealizable demand or a vision for some dreamed-of future. Ethics is rather the call to what is possible in the here and now because of what God's grace has already done in the here and now.

INTERPRETATIONS BY NEW TESTAMENT SCHOLARS

We now turn to NT scholars and ask the same basic question: How do they think we can get from there to here? In NT scholarship, just as in Ogletree, this issue cannot be discussed independently of that of eschatology, since throughout this century the decision about the relation of ethics and eschatol-

---

[23]Ibid., 90; italics added.

[24]Ibid., 175-206.

[25]Ibid., 182.

ogy has, in general, decisively determined the outcome of any decision about possible relevance. Everything depends upon the kind of eschatology chosen as the model.

One can call this relationship the legacy of Albert Schweitzer. As is well-known, Schweitzer popularized the importance of future eschatology for Jesus' thinking.[26] Not only did his thought structure base itself on a future kingdom of God, the *imminence* of this coming kingdom was the touchstone of his ideas. Jesus thus taught his intimate disciples rules for living in this brief period before the eruption of God's rule. Hence Jesus' ethics are irrelevant for contemporary persons. They are directed only towards a select group of people who had special roles to play in this brief time. They are, consequently, not aimed at general rules for a noneschatological age. Schweitzer's "interim ethics" thus relativized Jesus' teaching to a select group for a special period of time.

Ground was laid for a change in this view of ethics with the claim, popularized in this instance by C. H. Dodd and Joachim Jeremias, that Jesus' eschatology was in a crucial way one of the *present* inbreaking of God's power and love.[27] The possibility is thus opened that the ethic might be freed from the time constraints laid upon it by a Schweitzer. In turn this leads to the further possibility that the limitation to a select few might also be eliminated. Awareness that the eschatology of Paul and the Gospel of John also had present dimensions increased the scope of the release from a purely future-determined ethic (if the Gospel of John could be said to have an ethic). No one did—or could—deny the fact that many segments of the NT are completely future-oriented.

Of course such changes in the understanding of eschatology do not necessarily lead to a broadening of ethical perspective. Just as, according to Schweitzer, Jesus was wrong about the imminent coming, so he could have been wrong about its present inbreaking. That is, as long as the kingdom is in either view seen as primarily the cataclysmic, cosmic end of the world, Jesus could have been as much in error in his views of the presence of the kingdom as in a view that he held it to be imminent.

The final step was to argue that the present kingdom proclaimed by Jesus (and Paul and John) was primarily that of a *relationship* between God as King and persons as subjects and fellow inheritors with each other. Another way of stating the matter is to claim that the kingdom is a quality of life, or authentic

---

[26]Cf. his best known work, *The Quest of the Historical Jesus*, English translation published in 1910 from the German original, *Von Reimarus zu Wrede* (1906). J. Weiss, *Die Predigt Jesu vom Reiche Gottes* (1892), of course, preceded Schweitzer.

[27]Cf. C. H. Dodd, *The Parables of the Kingdom* (London: Nisbet, 1935), and J. Jeremias, *The Parables of Jesus* (New York: Scribner's, 1955).

existence, a possibility of new being once persons accept the reign of God over them.[28] In a final chapter in Dodd's *Parables of the Kingdom* the British scholar pointed in this direction, and of course Rudolf Bultmann has had many followers for a similar view. The person who has, in my judgment, created the most appropriate slogan is Dominic Crossan. We should talk, he claims, not about present eschatology but "permanent eschatology."[29] Life before God, or in the kingdom, is a possibility for anyone who turns in faith (understood as a quality of life or a perspective on reality) to the God proclaimed by Jesus.

Amos Wilder contributed importantly to this further movement with his book, *Eschatology and Ethics in the Teaching of Jesus*, first published in 1939.[30] Here the author claimed two things. First, eschatology in relation to ethics is a sanction (that is, a reason for acting in such a way) but was secondary to the primary sanction of the nature of God. Secondly, and most crucially, Wilder saw that the present dimension of Jesus' eschatology decisively changed the ethical dimension. The content of the ethic "is qualified by the dawn of the new age."[31] That is, the very *possibility* of acting rightly is given insofar as one lives now in the kingdom. Surrender to the kingdom of God "is the choice of *a greatly modified self*, since it is a self profoundly altered by the situation into which it has been plunged by the impact of the gospel."[32]

The implications of this interpretation are immense, since it would mean not only that eschatological ethics are relevant to a person today but in fact *are made possible* by participation in the present dynamic of God's reign over humankind. *Mutatis mutandis*, the same claim can be made for any ethics in the NT that rests on a view of the kingdom as a present reality. The door opens for relevancy not only for Jesus, but at least for Paul and the Gospel of John as well. The reflections of Ogletree about a "dialectic eschatology" are obviously to the point here.

Neither Wilder nor Bultmann, however, have laid Schweitzer to rest. Scholars still defend the validity of a futuristic eschatology in Jesus, and in Jack T. Sanders we have seen a recent defense of the implications for the rel-

---

[28]Many ways of expressing this understanding have, of course, been proposed. Perhaps the most popular has been that of "authentic existence," used by R. Bultmann. Cf. my own attempt at a description in *Paul for a New Day* (Philadelphia: Fortress, 1977) 21-38.

[29]Cf. Dodd, *Parables*, 195-210, and the moving statement in his *History and the Gospel* (London: Nisbet, 1938) 149-82. As Crossan describes his own view, "The thesis is that Jesus is proclaiming what might be termed *permanent eschatology*, the permanent presence of God as the one who challenges world and shatters its complacency repeatedly" (*In Parables* [New York: Harper, 1973] 26).

[30]New York: Harper, 1939.

[31]Ibid., 194.

[32]Ibid., 209, italics added.

evancy (or irrelevancy) of NT ethics raised years ago by Schweitzer.[33] Sanders, in his sweeping treatment of NT ethics, consistently defends the dependence of that ethics on a basically futuristic eschatology. This judgment leads Sanders to defend Schweitzer over against Wilder and Bultmann and to reach the same negative conclusions that Schweitzer did.

> To put the matter now most sharply, Jesus does not provide a valid ethics for today. His ethical teaching is interwoven with his imminent eschatology to such a degree that every attempt to separate the two and to draw out only the ethical thread invariably draws out also strands of the eschatology, so that both yarns only lie in a heap.[34]

Paul's ethic receives little more positive treatment, although Sanders does point out "Paul's fleeting denial of eschatology in favor of the *qualitative transcendence* of love."[35] And John's perspective so turns into an "insider" vs. "outsider" perspective that the real issue is not love but whether one comes to believe.[36]

Sanders's conclusion and an insight into his own concerns emerge in a pungent statement worth quoting at length.

> The ethical positions of the New Testament are the children of their own times and places, alien and foreign to this day and age. Amidst the ethical dilemmas which confront us, we are now at least relieved of the need or temptation to begin with Jesus, or the early church, or the NT, if we wish to develop coherent positions. *We are freed from bondage to that tradition*, and we are able to propose, with the author of the Epistle of James, that tradition and precedent must not be allowed to stand in the way of what is humane and right.[37]

The author is clear in his broad judgment that NT ethics in general, apart from certain secondary hints, is irrelevant to contemporary ethical discussion. Equally clear is his passion for justice, which comes out precisely in his declaration of liberation from bondage to what he considers to be an outmoded and timebound ethical system. To be free from the Bible means to be free for contemporary discussion based on our own decisions about what is "humane and right."

---

[33]Cf. Jack T. Sanders, *Ethics in the New Testament* (Philadelphia: Fortress, 1975). For a recent general defense of Schweitzer's eschatological views, cf. Richard H. Hiers, *Jesus and the Future* (Atlanta: John Knox, 1981).

[34]Sanders, *Ethics* 29.

[35]Ibid., 129.

[36]Ibid., 100.

[37]Ibid., 130; italics added.

Suppose, however, that Sanders is wrong in his conclusions about eschatology (as I think he is). Suppose that there is an important present dimension to eschatological understanding in much of the NT. Suppose this means that we are in fact obligated to "begin with Jesus," or Paul or John. Does this mean that we are thus in bondage to some outmoded system, or does the seriousness with which we may feel obligated to consider NT ethics in fact give us a true liberation to pursue what is "humane and right"? These are questions to ponder.

A survey nearly contemporary to that of Sanders has been made by the British scholar, J. L. Houlden.[38] Although he shares with Sanders some of the same concerns, his approach and evaluation are sufficiently different to merit a brief discussion in this essay. Houlden begins with the writers of the NT, then discusses certain ethical issues, and only at the end of his historical study brings Jesus into the picture. This structure is due to the author's uncertainty about how much can be said confidently about Jesus' teaching, an uncertainty, of course, shared by most critical scholars today.

Paul presents, according to Houlden, two approaches to the moral life that are basically inconsistent, each based on a different view of eschatology. On the one hand there is emphasis on the presence of salvation, produced by God's act in Christ. "The prime result of that act, as far as Paul was concerned, was not to produce a new moral imperative but rather a new state of life."[39] "Only if a man ceases to be a slave to morality and becomes the slave of Christ (1 Cor. vii, 21f) can the spirit enable him to live in freedom and love."[40] On the other hand, Paul still sees the kingdom as imminent future reality, and in cases he can thus appeal to specific rules and regulations, sometimes even to the Jewish law. Houlden seems to suggest, however, that this second mode of dealing with ethics is not as central to Paul's theological program as is the former.

Houlden judges the Johannine writings as severely as does Sanders. The in-group stance of the community is so prevailing that even the new commandment of love is only for insiders. "Love seems almost like a huddling together for warmth and safety in the face of the world" is his comment on the Gospel itself.[41] And of the authors of the Johannine corpus as a whole he can

---

[38]J. L. Houlden, *Ethics and the New Testament* (New York: Oxford University, 1977), first published in 1973.

[39]Ibid., 31.

[40]Ibid., 34.

[41]Ibid., 39.

conclude: "No New Testament writer has less interest in the sanctifying of ordinary life than these."[42]

This scholar seems to think that Jesus made a radical break with the law—
since it is not in laws that one can capture the demand of God—and that he
lived out of an urgent sense of the coming kingdom, although the author does
not seem to think it possible to determine just what sort of eschatology Jesus
proclaimed. His interpretation is summed up in the statement, "The Church
had to build up the rule-book which Jesus had failed to provide, and thereby it
imperilled its hold on the clarity of Jesus' message—which was radically dis-
trustful of all such documents."[43]

In his concluding chapter Houlden draws three conclusions about the issue
of relevancy.[44] 1) The teaching of the NT is timebound and speaks to its own
age and situation, not our own. 2) The real legacy lies in its proclamation of
"a certain style of relationship with God," a phrase which at least leads in the
direction of the sense of the new being inaugurated by God in the Christ
event.[45] 3) This legacy actually gives us freedom from NT ethical judgments—indeed may in fact demand it for our own day. "It is arguable that to
be true to the deepest convictions of the leading New Testament writers, and
more, to be faithful to the Lord who lay behind them, we need to be emanci-
pated from the letter of their teaching."[46]

CONCLUDING REFLECTIONS

What may we learn from this all too selective and superficial journey
through recent work by both ethicists and biblical scholars? While each has
made unique contributions, I want here to highlight the things they tend to
share in common.

1. All agree in what on the surface is a negative conclusion: it is not easy
to get from there to here. No one offers a simple, positive methodology of pro-
ceeding from NT judgments to present problems. As Gustafson has pointed
out, even the apparently simple ways turn out to be not as simple upon reflection. While the NT is not to be ignored, except perhaps in the extreme case of
Sanders's view, it is not the only source of moral insight. It may even be at
times an inadequate guide, *based on its own deepest theological insights* (so
Houlden).

---

[42]Ibid., 41.

[43]Ibid., 114.

[44]Ibid., 115-25.

[45]Ibid., 117.

[46]Ibid., 120.

2. All think it necessary to state first and foremost that the NT dicta are aimed at their own time and cultural *Sitz im Leben*, not our own. Obviously the authors of our documents had no vision about problems of overpopulation and ecology. Even on matters that do have "then and now" parallels, for example the perennial question of the relation between male and female, it is invalid to spring the insights of a Jesus or a Paul loose from their own location in time and space. To transfer such first century judgments to our own very different time and experience without great care and selectivity is dangerous.[47]

3. This leads to a third agreement, that within the NT ethical judgments are diverse, at times contradictory, at times stem from different theological functions. Thus, even if we could devise a way to get from there to here, we would first have to determine from *which* "there" we wished to begin. The criterion we would choose for this determination is most likely to come from outside the NT itself. The implication in such a case is that the use of the NT is not really essential (since determination for what is correct has already been made from the outside) or is at least problematic.

4. With the exception of Gustafson, all the thinkers discussed insert eschatology prominently into their discussions. Even here there is complexity, since there are various interpretations of the eschatology of the NT. Decision about eschatology clearly impinges upon views of ethical pronouncements. I will say more about this.

5. Finally, the seemingly most discouraging conclusion. Given the complexity with which these scholars view the situation, none of them seems to offer *any* clear methodological structure by which to proceed from there to here. Gustafson concludes that NT insights are one kind among many to be considered, but he does not suggest a certain way to isolate and utilize this document—that is, what place it has and what role it plays as one among many. Ogletree introduces several contemporary ethical theories but does not seem to suggest that any of them provide a methodological tool to close the gap. Houlden thinks that NT theological principles may suggest that at times we reject specific judgments in the NT, but he does not outline a series of steps to show how this might be done with clarity and consistency.

In short, if such thinkers are to be taken as indicative of the best kinds of thinking possible today, as I think they are, the questioner is left, when all is said and done, with no sure guidelines about getting from there to here. We are finally left in the uncomfortable position of facing the present problems, looking over our shoulder at the past, yet ultimately urged towards that abyss of awful freedom and responsibility which forces on us the necessity to make

---

[47]Cf. my conclusions on the issue of homosexuality in Scroggs, *Homosexuality and the New Testament* (Philadelphia: Fortress, 1983) 123-29.

a decision without the comfort of knowing that God agrees with us. Perhaps the only solace we have is that which Paul gives us, as I have paraphrased 1 Cor. 13:12 elsewhere: "It is more important to be aware that we are graced by God than it is to be sure we know all the answers."[48]

As I try to think through that abyss, I try to allow myself to be led by the following steps, which might be seen as a process. Of course these steps do not provide the clarity we would like to possess. They are, however, the best I can present, and I offer them to the reader for whatever heuristic value they may have.

1. I agree, as I think most scholars would, that the NT must first be interpreted in terms of what it *said*, not in terms of what it *says*. The ethical pronouncements must be rigorously pursued in the context of the cultural and religious situation of the time of writing. Careful attention must be paid to similarities and differences between that situation and ours today.

2. The questions must always be asked (even if they cannot always be adequately answered): On what theological principles or realities are the ethical judgments based? Can we accept those principles today? Would we draw the same conclusion as did the NT author, leading from those same principles?

3. The relation between ethics and eschatology can never be avoided, but the issue, as already suggested, is very complex. One relation can be that of the sanction of reward and punishment. In such a case the pronouncement, the *content* of which may have been arrived at completely independently of eschatological expectations, may be evaluated apart from its particular relation to eschatology. If, on the other hand, the relation is based on the demand, "live this way in order to plan for or prepare others for the coming, future kingdom," then the connection cannot be severed. We have then a true "interim ethic." It would be my judgment that there are actually few instances of a true interim ethic in the NT.[49]

4. An eschatologically influenced ethical statement bears most *potential* relevance for our time *if and in so far as* the eschatology is pronounced a present reality. A certain performance is in this case asked for not *in order* to enter a future kingdom but *because* that kingdom, bringing with it a transformed self, is already a force within the present order. It is here that, as we have seen,

---

[48]Ibid., 129.

[49]One place where it is common to point to such an interim ethic is 1 Corinthians 7, where to buttress some of his judgments about the relations between male and female he writes the sentences in verses 29-31, the famous "live as though" passage, with its conclusion, "For the form of this world is passing away." I have argued, however, that the real sanction for the preference for the unmarried state lies in verses 32-35, which highlights the importance of undivided attention, most possible for the single person, to the community of faith; cf. Scroggs, "Paul and the Eschatological Woman," *JAAR* 40 (1972) 296-97.

major differences of interpretation still exist. I can only affirm that I see in Jesus, Paul, and the Gospel of John strong claims that such a present kingdom is in existence.

My statement assumes that not all ethical pronouncements in the NT are based on a sense of the presence of the kingdom. The implication is clear. Ethical statements based on a claim that the kingdom is a present reality are to be taken more earnestly than statements that appear to operate out of a belief in an entirely future kingdom. I am aware that such a decision has immense exegetical and hermeneutical dangers, but I am convinced that we need to begin with this judgment, whatever modifications or refinements may be necessary later in the process.

This is, after all, but another variation in the hermeneutical principle, used by Protestants since Luther, of the "analogy of faith." One obvious application can be seen in the area of male-female relationships of such vital concern to Frank Stagg. In Paul, where the sense of the presence of the kingdom lived out in justification by grace through faith is strong, there is a basic affirmation of the *equality* of male and female. In the deutero-Pauline writings, the importance of the presence of the kingdom as an existential reality is greatly diminished, if not often completely eclipsed by the judgment that it is future. Is it an accident that in these later writings the *subordination* of female to male is an important theme?

5. I am prepared then to take the next step, that this present kingdom is a "world switching" into a new reality, of which the self as transformed is part. That is, there is a new quality of being due to the "radical perceptual shift," enabling one to see God and the possible relationship with Her in a new light.[50] This new quality of existence is possible to all today who are willing to live out of that new relationship. Since part of this transformed self is, according to Paul, a renewed perception of thinking and evaluating what is real, the ethical statement may itself stem out of the new self in the kingdom of God.[51] Thus the presence of the kingdom of God, in the day of the NT and in our own, refers not to some cosmic manifestation of God's power but to a new mode of being made possible through coming to understand God and his will anew.

Ethical statements made on the basis of the experience of this new mode of being thus have a claim on our consideration. Not only may they show us what is now possible to the person in faith, they may also bestow new insight

---

[50]Cf. D. Batson, C. Beker, M. Clark, *Commitment Without Ideology* (Philadelphia: Pilgrim, 1973), for the notion of "radical perceptual shift," and my discussion in *Paul for a New Day*, 25-26.

[51]Cf. my discussion in *Paul for a New Day*, 60, and the more detailed description in Scroggs, "New Being: Renewed Mind: New Perception. Paul's View of the Source of Ethical Insight," *Chicago Theological Seminary Register* 72 (1982) 5-10.

into God's will for individual and community. In my judgment these steps do help us move towards isolating those NT ethical statements that may have potential relevance for our own time. Yet things are never simple. We first must confront the concreteness of the cultural situation of the time of the NT, and in addition the always only partly realized transformation of the author of such statements. Paul, for example, may have made his ethical suggestions (which are rarely prescriptions, despite popular views to the contrary) on the basis of his transformed self and transformed mind.[52] He still is a finite person living in a finite world. How do we know that what he thinks can be helpful in our own ethical deliberations, even if his applications may have seemed to him legitimate in his own time and space?

6. I think that the principle of analogy is imperative at this point, even though the cautions of a Gustafson must be heeded. *If* the situation of a Paul is analogous to a situation in today's world, then his ethical claim should be heard and used to inform our current discussions.

7. Finally, however, even that step may fail or appear uncertain. If every situation is unique, then the principle of analogy may not seem to hold entirely. We have, I believe, at this point gone as far as we can go from there to here. If the steps enumerated above—or some other, perhaps better series—fail us at the last state of reflection, we may have to face that abyss in which we must decide without the comfort of knowing that God agrees with us.

Two things we should here keep in mind. The first is that we must always be open to rethink the biblical message, most particularly when it goes against our own judgments and insights into our ethical situation. The second is that we ultimately *do* have to assert our own freedom and responsibility, *even when we do feel guided by biblical insight*. This means, on the one hand, that we can in Christian freedom go our own way independently of the biblical statements, perhaps at times even contrary to them. On the other, it means we have to take responsibility for our decisions. Whether we go our own way or follow a NT imperative, we must go in fear and trembling. All our decisions are imperfect, shot through with deep-seated and partly unconscious self-motivations. Thus at the end of our journey we face both freedom and the need for forgiveness. Fortunately, believers in Christ trust the promise and the reality of both.

---

[52]Cf. my reference to Hengel in note 6. Of course, the reverse can hold, that contemporary use is *not* possible if the analogy does not fit, a conclusion I draw with regard to homosexuality as understood in the NT, cf. *Homosexuality*, 123-29.

PAUL'S UNDERSTANDING OF THE HOLY SPIRIT: THE EVIDENCE OF 1 CORINTHIANS 12-14

CHARLES H. TALBERT
WAKE FOREST UNIVERSITY
WINSTON-SALEM, NORTH CAROLINA 27109

In this essay I propose to give a close reading of three problematic chapters related to the experience of the Spirit in the Corinthian community.[1] Rather than analyze every difficult detail in depth, my aim will be to trace the train of thought in the whole, saving until the end a summary description of the positions of both the Corinthians and Paul.

At 12:1 Paul returns to the questions raised in the Corinthian letter (7:1; 7:25; 8:1):[2] "Now concerning the spiritual gifts" (14:1 predisposes one to translate "spiritual gifts" instead of "spiritual persons").[3] This is a topic discussed by the apostle elsewhere in Rom 12:6-8 (cf. 1 Thess 5:19-22), by the

---

[1]W. O. Carver, *The Acts of the Apostles* (Nashville: Sunday School Board, Southern Baptist Convention, 1916) 26, whose judgment of the Pentecostal experience of his day ("the modern gibberish of ignorant fanatics") made it impossible for him to read the parts of the New Testament dealing with the Holy Spirit correctly, is the backdrop against which to read Frank Stagg's *The Holy Spirit Today* (Nashville: Broadman, 1974), an influential volume in current Southern Baptist life. This essay indirectly raises the question of whether or not Stagg has understood Paul.

[2]John C. Hurd, Jr., *The Origin of 1 Corinthians* (London: SPCK, 1965) 63-74.

[3]Hans Conzelmann, *1 Corinthians* (Philadelphia: Fortress, 1975) 204. For the opposite point of view, see Walter Schmithals, *Gnosticism in Corinth* (Nashville: Abingdon, 1971) 171-72.

Pauline school in Eph 4:11, and by 1 Pet 4:10-11. In chapters 12-14 Paul treats the third in a series of matters relating to corporate worship (A—11:2-16; B—11:17-34; A¹—chaps 12-14).[4] These three chapters consist of an initial statement of the criterion by which truly Christian religious experience can be discerned (12:2-3), followed by an ABA¹ pattern:[5] A—Spiritual gifts (12:4-30); B—Proper motivation in manifesting manifesting the gifts (12:31-14:1a); A¹—Spiritual gifts (14:1b-40). Each of these components must be examined in turn.

In 1 Cor 12:2-3, Paul gives the Christological criterion for evaluating any alleged gift. He is concerned at the very beginning to distinguish what is and what is not Christian religious experience. Two examples, one pagan and the other Jewish, show that not all religious experience is Christian. On the pagan side: "You know that when pagans you were regularly led astray to dumb idols as you were moved" (cf. Lucian, *Dialogi Mortuorum* 19:1). On the Jewish side: "No one speaking by the Spirit of God says, 'Jesus is anathema' " (as certain Jews did in the synagogues—cf. Justin, *Dialogue* 16:4, 47:4; 96:2; 137:2).[6] As in Deut 13:1-5, Paul's criterion is the content of one's confession: "No one is able to say, 'Jesus is Lord,' except by the Holy Spirit" (12:3b). In the early church a variety of criteria were employed to distinguish truly Christian religious experience:[7] (a) Matt 7:6 and Didache 11:8-12 specify ethical conduct as the test; (b) Hermas, *Command*, 11:7-16 and 3 Corinthians 3 make their judgment on ecclesiastical grounds; while (c) 1 John 4:1-3 and 1 Cor 12:2-3 employ a Christological criterion. Both pagans and Jews have religious experience, Paul acknowledges, but only that which points to Jesus as Lord is deemed by the apostle to be due to the Holy Spirit (cf. John 15:26). Within these boundaries, Paul accepts the gifts as manifestations of the Spirit.

A, 12:4-30, deals with the variety of gifts in the one body. Once again the pattern is ABA¹: A—the variety of gifts (12:4-11); B—the one body (12:12-27); A¹—the variety of gifts (12:28-30). 12:4-11, A, is a thought unit held together by an inclusion (verses 4 and 11, "the same Spirit"). Not only is the term "Spirit" the dominant word in the paragraph, it is also the linking word

---

[4]Jerome Murphy-O'Connor, *1 Corinthians* (Wilmington DE: Michael Glazier, 1979) 103-104.

[5]On the importance of the ABA¹ pattern in Paul, see John J. Collins, "Chiasmus, the 'ABA' Pattern and the Text of Paul," in *Studiorum Paulinorum Congressus Internationalis Catholicus* (Rome: Biblical Institute Press, 1963) 2:575-84. On the use of this rhetorical technique generally in antiquity, see John W. Welch, ed., *Chiasmus in Antiquity: Structure, Analyses, Exegesis* (Hildesheim: Gerstenberg, 1981).

[6]J. M. D. Derrett, "Cursing Jesus (1 Cor 12:3): The Jews as Religious Persecutors," *NTS* 21 (1975) 544-54.

[7]Joseph Lienhard, "On Discernment of Spirits in the Early Church," *Theol Stud* 41 (1980) 509-14.

that ties 12:4-11 to the previous unit, 12:2-3. The theme of 12:4-11 is the variety of gifts.[8] Included here are the utterance of wisdom (12:8; cf. 1 Kings 3:16-28, Isa 11:2, Lk 21:15, Acts 6:10), the utterance of knowledge (12:8; John 14:26), faith (12:9; not saving faith nor faith as a fruit of the Spirit, Gal 5:22, but "faith that moves mountains," 1 Cor 13:2, Matt 17:20), gifts of healing (12:9), the working of miracles (15:10; cf. John 14:12, Acts 4:29-30), prophecy (12:10; cf. Jer 1:9, 2 Chron 20:14-15, Joel 2:28-29, Acts 2:16-18), the ability to distinguish between spirits (12:10; cf. 1 Kings 22, 1 John 4:1), various kinds of tongues (12:10; Acts 10:44-45, 19:6), the interpretation of tongues (12:10). "All these are inspired by one and the same Spirit, who apportions to each one individually as he wills" (12:11).

Note first that this is not the same list that appears in Rom 12:6-8 (prophecy, service, teaching, exhortation, contributing, giving aid, acts of mercy). It is clear from such a comparison that both unusual and more usual types of action, for Paul, fall within the sphere of the gifts of the Spirit.

Note second that such phenomena continued in the patristic period, at least in some circles. Hermas, *Parable*, 9:13, sets the tone: "If you bear his name but possess not his power, it will be in vain that you bear his name." Several representative sources continue this theme: (a) Eusebius, *Ecclesiastical History*, 3:37, 39, tells how in the time of Trajan prophecy and miracles continued. (b) Justin, *Dialogue*, 39, says, "For one receives the spirit of understanding, another of counsel, another of strength, another of healing, another of foreknowledge, another of teaching, and another of the fear of God"; in 82, he says: "the prophetic gifts remain with us, even to the present time."[9] (c) Eusebius, 5:3:4, tells how in the time of Marcus Aurelius many wonderful works of the grace of God were still being wrought up to that time in many churches. (d) Also in the time of Marcus Aurelius, Irenaeus, *Against Heresies*, 2:32:4, relates that "some . . . drive out devils . . . others have foreknowledge of things to come: they see visions and utter prophetic expressions. Others still heal the sick by laying their hands upon them, and they are made whole. Yea, moreover, as I have said, the dead even have been raised up, and remained among us for many years. And what shall I say more? It is not possible to name the number of the gifts which the church, scattered throughout

---

[8]For a discussion of the individual gifts within the larger context of Christian mysticism, see Harvey D. Egan, *Christian Mysticism: The Future of a Tradition* (New York: Pueblo Publishing Company, 1984) chapter 8, "Christian Mysticism and Unusual Phenomena." Cf. also G. T. Montague, *The Spirit and His Gifts* (New York: Paulist, 1974), and Arnold Bittlinger, *Gifts and Graces: A Commentary on 1 Corinthians 12-14* (London: Hodder & Stoughton, 1967).

[9]Unless otherwise indicated, citations from the early fathers will be taken from the *Ante-Nicene Fathers*.

the whole world, has received from God." In 5:6:1, Irenaeus tells about "many brethren in the church, who possess prophetic gifts, and who through the Spirit speak all kinds of languages" (cf. 5:16, 17 on prophecy). (e) Tertullian, *A Treatise on the Soul*, 9; *Against Marcion*, 5:8. (f) Eusebius, 6:9, for the time of Caracalla; cf. also 6:43:11, 14 (52 exorcists in the Roman church of that time). (g) Origen, *De Principiis*, Preface, 3; *Against Celsus*, 1:46, says: "And there are still preserved among Christians traces of that Holy Spirit which appeared in the form of a dove. They expel evil spirits, and perform many cures, and foresee certain events." (h) Novatian, *De Trinitate*, 29; (i) Eusebius, 10:4:66 (about events in his own time). (j) *Apostolic Constitutions*, 8:1. (k) Cyril of Jerusalem, *Catechesis*, 16:15-16; (l) Gregory the Great, *Moralia*, 9:13, 20, asks: "Which one of us does not think himself close to God when he sees himself overwhelmed with favors from on high, when he receives the gift of prophecy, ... the grace of curing the sick?" Given this evidence, it is clear that Paul is not speaking about something that was restricted to Corinth or to the first century.

Note third that most of the gifts mentioned here are Christologically grounded: utterance of wisdom (Luke 20:20-26); utterance of knowledge (Luke 7:39-50); faith (John 11:41-42); gifts of healing (Luke 7:22); working of miracles (Luke 9:10-17); prophecy (Luke 18:31-33 with Luke 22-24; Luke 11:13 with Acts 1:14 and chap. 2); ability to distinguish between spirits (Luke 4:1-3, 9:49-50). Note fourth that this diversity of gifts is not only from the one Spirit but is also for the common good (12:7).

In 12:12-17, B, a unit held together by an inclusion (12:12 and 27, body/members/Christ), Paul focuses on the organic unity of the Christian community. To do this, he employs a fable of the body and its limbs that was widely used in antiquity (Livy 2:32, tells how Menenius Agrippa used it with the plebeians in Rome; Epictetus, *Dissertations* 2:10:3, shows how the Stoics used it for political life; Midrash Tehillim on Ps 39:2 employs it in a Jewish context). "For just as the body is one and has many members, and all the members of the body, though many, are one body, so it is with Christ" (12:12). Christ here is not the name of an individual, Jesus, but of the community which derives its existence and identity from the individual. Just as in the Old Testament Israel could serve as the name of an individual (Gen 32:28) and of a people, so in Paul the name Christ is used both for the individual (1 Cor 2:2, Rom 5:17) and for the Christian community (1 Cor 15:22, 2 Cor 5:19). The Christian community, Paul is saying, is like the human body. It is an organic unity but has a multiplicity of parts.

This organic unity is created by the Spirit. "For in one Spirit we were all baptized into one body . . . and all were made to drink of one Spirit" (12:13). Two images are used here. The first is "baptism in the Spirit." The expression is that used in the Gospels (Luke 3:16, John 1:33) and Acts (1:5, 11:16) and with the same meaning.[10] Here the Spirit is not the baptizer but the one in whom all are baptized. One is immersed in the Spirit. The other image is that of drinking the Spirit.[11] Although the verb is different, the thought is the same as that in John 7:37-39 (cf. John 4:14). Taken together, the two pictures say that the Spirit is both within and all around believers. In the Pauline churches, this experience usually occurred in the context of proclamation (Gal 3:1-5, 1 Cor 2:1-5, 1 Thess 1:5) much like the narrative of Acts 10:44-48 relates about Peter and Cornelius.[12] It is this experience of the Spirit that incorporates people into the Christian community.

This organic unity demands a view of Christian diversity of gifts that fits with the oneness of the body of Christ rather than detracting from it. "The eye cannot say to the hand, 'I have no need of you' nor again the head to the feet, 'I have no need of you' " (12:21). "If one member suffers, all suffer together; if one member is honored, all rejoice together" (12:26).

In A[1], 12:28-30, Paul returns to his emphasis on the varieties of gifts. In 12:28 his list is different in part from that in 12:4-11. Here he speaks of apostles, prophets (1 Cor 12:10, Rom 12:6), teachers (Rom 12:7), workers of miracles (1 Cor 12:10), healers (1 Cor 12:9), helpers (Rom 12:8 ?), administrators, speakers in various kinds of tongues (1 Cor 12:10). In 12:29-30 there are seven rhetorical questions, each one demanding a negative response. "Are all apostles?" No. "Are all prophets?" No. "Are all teachers?" No. "Do all work miracles?" No. "Do all possess gifts of healing?" No. "Do all speak with tongues?" No. "Do all interpret?" No. The gifts are diverse and not every Christian is a recipient of all (cf. Rom 12:6, "Having gifts that differ according to the grace given to us, let us use them"). Not only are there diverse gifts, but also different people are used by the Spirit to deliver the different gifts for the common good.

1 Cor 12:31-14:1a, B in the larger pattern, focuses on the proper motivation in manifesting the gifts. The unit is introduced in 12:31a with a sentence that can be translated either as an imperative ("But earnestly desire the higher gifts," so RSV) or as an indicative ("But you are are eagerly desiring," so NIV margin). Two arguments support the indicative reading.[13] First, Paul distinguishes between the gifts of the Spirit and the fruit of the Spirit (Gal 5:22-23, "But the fruit of the Spirit is love, joy, peace, patience, kindness, goodness,

---

[10]F. F. Bruce, *1 & 2 Corinthians* (Grand Rapids: Eerdmans, 1971) 120.

[11]E. R. Rogers, "EPOTISTHĒMEN Again," *NTS* (1983) 139-41.

[12]This is the lasting contribution of David J. Lull, *The Spirit in Galatia* (Chico, Cal.: Scholars Press, 1980). This, of course, undermines any necessary link between water baptism and the gift of the Holy Spirit.

[13]Gerhard Iber, "Zum Verständnis von 1 Cor 12:31," *ZNW* 54 (1963) 43-52; J. Murphy-O'Connor, *1 Corinthians*, 122.

faithfulness, gentleness, self-control"). If one reads an imperative, "Earnestly desire the higher gifts," then Paul seems to be saying his readers should strive for love as the higher gift. For the apostle, however, love is a fruit of the Spirit, not a gift of the Spirit. Second, in chapter 12 it seems that the Corinthians were in fact distinguishing between the greater and the lesser gifts and were coveting the greater. It seems also that Paul had urged them to be content with the gift(s) apportioned them. If one reads an imperative in 12:31a, Paul would then be reinforcing such distinctions and their quest. If one reads an indicative, "But you are eagerly desiring the higher gifts," then the apostle would merely be reporting the sad state of affairs in Corinth. The Corinthian spirituals were interested in gifts not for the common good (12:7) but for their own personal status. Their motivation in manifesting the spiritual gifts was wrong. Paul, therefore, responds: "And I will show you a still more excellent way" (12:31b). Chapter 13, then, focuses on love as the motivation for applying the gifts.

1 Cor 13:1-13 is an aretalogy of love (cf. a similar aretalogy of truth in 1 Esdras 4:34-40)[14] that falls into an ABA[1] pattern: A—the superiority of love (13:1-3); B—the characterization of love (13:4-7); and A[1]—the superiority of love (13:8-13).[15] 13:1-3, A, is organized around a threefold repetition of the refrain, "If I . . . but have not love, I am nothing." This section speaks of the incompleteness of tongues, prophecy, faith, and sacrifice without love as motivation. 13:4-7, B, characterizes love in three ways: first, what loves does in two positive descriptions ("Love is patient and kind"); second, what love does not do in eight negatives ("love is not jealous or boastful; it is not arrogant or rude. Love does not insist on its own way; it is not irritable or resentful; it does not rejoice at wrong"); and third, what love does in five positives ("rejoices in the right. Love bears all things, believes all things, hopes all things, endures all things"). 13:8-13, A[1], resumes the theme of the superiority of love, emphasizing its permanence ("Love never ends"—13:8a; "so faith, hope, love abide"—13:13a) over against the transient nature of prophecy ("as for prophecies, they will pass away"—13:8b), of tongues ("as for tongues, they will cease"—13:8c), and of knowledge ("as for knowledge, it will pass away"—13:8d).[16] The time for the passing of the gifts is "when the perfect comes" (13:10), that is, at the parousia.[17] Love, then, stands supreme as the more ex-

---

[14]Conzelmann, *1 Corinthians*, 218.

[15]Nils Johansson, "1 Cor 13 and 1 Cor 14," *NTS* 10 (1964) 383-92, makes a good case for the unity of chapters 12-14.

[16]Beda Rigaux, *The Letters of St. Paul* (Chicago: Franciscan Herald Press, 1968) 135.

[17]Ronald Cottle, "Tongues Shall Cease," *Pneuma* 1 (1979) 43-49; Wayne A. Grudem, *The Gift of Prophecy in 1 Corinthians* (Washington, D. C.: University Press of America, 1983).

cellent motivation for the manifestation of spiritual gifts. The unit concludes with the Pauline exhortation: "Make love your aim" (14:1a). In saying this, the apostle does not aim to replace the spiritual gifts with love (cf. 14:1— "make love your aim" followed by "zealously seek the spiritual gifts") but to undergird them with this fruit of the Spirit.

1 Cor 14:1b-40, A[1], returns to the focus on spiritual gifts. This unit is held together by an inclusion (14:1 and 39, "seek to prophesy"). It falls into two sections, (1) 14:1b-19, a Pauline thesis in two parts with supporting arguments, and (2) 14:20-36, two Corinthian assertions followed by their Pauline responses, after which comes a concluding summary (14:37-40). (1) In the first section, 14:1b-19, the thesis is formulated in 14:1b-5: (a) in public worship, prophecy is preferable to tongues (14:1b, 5a,b), (b) unless the tongues are interpreted (14:5b).[18] The ultimate test of comparison is benefit for the church (14:5b—"so that the church may be edified"; cf. 12:7, "for the common good"). What follows are two clusters of arguments (14:6-12 and 14:13-19).

In the first cluster there are three arguments in favor of prophecy in public worship (14:6-12).[19] First, if Paul came speaking only tongues, the Corinthians would not benefit (14:6; cf. 1 Cor 15:1-11). Second, if musical instruments do not communicate unless their sounds are arranged in an intelligible pattern, then the Corinthians should not expect to communicate in church unless their speech is intelligible to others (14:7-9). Third, if language is not understood, people are foreigners to each other (14:10-12). Throughout these three arguments the social concern of the apostle has been uppermost. Hence the cluster is concluded: "strive to excel in building up the church" (14:12b).

In the second cluster there are three arguments in favor of the interpretation of tongues in public worship (14:13-19).[20] 14:13 sets forth the theme: "he who speaks in a tongue should pray for the power to interpret." First, Paul argues, since what is said in tongues is not framed by the mind, nothing is communicated to others present at worship (14:14-15). Second, language that is not intelligible to all in public worship prevents the other Christians from responding with their "Amen" (14:16-17). Third, Paul's apostolic example is to be considered. "I thank God that I speak in tongues more than you all; never-

---

[18]Conzelmann, *1 Corinthians*, 235 says: "speaking with tongues can also be equally valuable—when it is interpreted, and thus acquires the same function as prophecy." A. Robertson and A. Plummer, *First Epistle of St. Paul to the Corinthians*, 2d ed. (Edinburgh: T. & T. Clark, 1914) 307, translate: "with this exception, unless he interpret." J. W. MacGorman, "Glossolalic Error and Its Correction: 1 Cor 12-14," *Rev Exp* 80 (1983) 397, fails to see that this second part of the thesis derives not only from the phrase but also from the context of chapter 14.

[19]J. Murphy O'Connor, *1 Corinthians*, 128-29.

[20]Ibid., 129-30.

theless, *in church* I would rather speak five words with my mind, in order to instruct others, than ten thousand words in a tongue" (14:18-19). Throughout these three arguments is the same social concern noted in the previous cluster. What is said in church is to be intelligible to all present. If tongues are used, therefore, they must be interpreted (14:13). In corporate worship uninterpreted tongues are inferior to prophecy as a vehicle for church edification.

(2) In the second section, 14:20-36, there are two Corinthian assertions followed in each case by their Pauline response. Prior to the two dialogue parts is the apostolic admonition: "Brethren, do not be children in your thinking . . . in thinking be mature." The first Corinthian assertion and Pauline reply come in 14:21-25.[21] The Corinthian assertion is found in 14:21-22. It consists of a quotation from scripture (Isa 28:11-12, "By men of strange tongues and by the lips of foreigners will I speak to this people, and even then they will not listen to me, says the Lord") followed by its interpretation in two stages: Thus, (a) tongues are a sign not for believers but for unbelievers,[22] (b) while prophecy is not for unbelievers but for believers.

Paul responds in 14:23-25, dealing with the two stages of the Corinthian interpretation of Isaiah 28 with two illustrative situations, perhaps out of their experience. (a) "If, therefore, the whole church assembles and all speak in tongues, and outsiders or unbelievers enter, will they not say that you are mad?" (14:23)[23] (b) "But if all prophesy, and an unbeliever or outsider enters, he is convicted by all, he is called to account by all, the secrets of his heart are disclosed; and so, falling on his face, he will worship God and declare that God is really among you." Such a reading both makes sense of what otherwise seems to be contradictory and fits the sense of the chapter as a whole. In this context, prophecy functions to disclose the secrets of the human heart, to produce conviction of sin, and to lead to a vindication both of God and of the Christian community (cf. John 16:7-11, Acts of John 56-57).

---

[21]B. C. Johanson, "Tongues, A Sign for Unbelievers?: A Structural and Exegetical Study of 1 Corinthians 14:20-25," *NTS* 25 (1979) 180-203.

[22]The reason the Corinthians held to such a position may have been that in antiquity there is evidence that the sure sign of an inspired speaker was that the deity authenticated the message previously delivered in an understandable language by means of tongues. See T. W. Gillespie, "A Pattern of Prophetic Speech in First Corinthians," *JBL* 97 (1978) 74-95.

[23]That is, the non-Christian world will identify the Christian community with the ecstatic pagan cults in which ritual madness was highly desirable. Paul asks, "Is this what you really want?" See Richard and Catherine Kroeger, "An Inquiry into Evidence of Maenadism in the Corinthian Congregation," *SBL 1978 Seminar Papers*, ed. P. J. Achtemeier (Missoula: Scholars Press, 1978) 2:331.

Prophecy was a phenomenon found in both the Greco-Roman and Jewish traditions in antiquity.[24] The pagan world had its oracular places and persons just as the Jewish heritage did. Early Christians understood prophecy within the church as a continuation or renewal of the prophecy of ancient Israel (Luke 1-2, 7:26, 7:39, Acts 2:16-21). When Justin Martyr said, "the prophetic gifts remain with us even to the present time" (*Dialogue* 82), he was expressing a widespread Christian belief. References to early Christian prophets and prophecies are extensive: 1 Thess 5:20, 1 Cor 12-14, Rom 12:4-6; Eusebius, *Ecclesiastical History* 3:5:3, refers to a prophecy telling Christians in Jerusalem to move to Pella; Eph 3:5, 4:11, 1 Tim 1:18, 4:14, Acts 11:27-28, 13:1-3, 15:22, 32, 19:6, 21:4, 9, 10-11, Rev 11:10, 18, 16:6, 18:20, 24, 22:6, 9, Didache 10:7, 11:3, 7-11, 13:1-6, 15:1-2, Ignatius, *Phil* 7:1-2, Hermas, *Command* 11:7, 12, 15, 16, Martyrdom of Polycarp 5:2, 12;3, Odes of Solomon 42:6, Quadratus (so Eusebius 3:37:1); Melito of Sardis (so Eusebius 4:26-20); Ammia of Philadelphia (so Eusebius 5:17:3-4). This early Christian prophecy was not just preaching and teaching but was regarded as a supernatural gift. According to Paul, it was a gift given to an individual (1 Cor 14:30); it had a spontaneous quality (14:30); it did not force one to speak against one's will (14:30, 32a); it enabled the prophet to know something from a divine perspective (14:24-25); it functioned for evangelism (14:24-25), for upbuilding, encouragement, and consolation of the church (14:3), as well as for learning (14:31); it was to cease at the parousia (13:8,10). Just as in ancient Israel so in the early church, false prophets and prophecy became a problem: 2 Thess 2:2, Matt 24:11, 23-24, 7:15-23, Mark 13:22, 1 John 4:1-3, Rev 2:20, 16:13, 19:20, 20:10, Didache 11:8-12, 13:1-7, Hermas, *Command* 11:7, the Gnostic Marcus (so Irenaeus, *Against Heresies* 1:13:3-4), Montanism (so Eusebius 5:16:6-9), Lucian, *Peregrinus* 11-13, Acts of Thomas 79, *Apostolic Constitutions* 8:2:1. Because of the problems with false prophecy, the gift of prophecy itself eventually fell into disuse and sometimes disrepute.

The New Testament speaks about two different phenomena with the label "tongues": (1) xenolalia (Acts 2), and (2) glossolalia (1 Cor 12, 14). In the former case, to speak in other tongues (Acts 2:4) is a gift of the Spirit (2:4, 17-18) that enables people listening to hear in their own language (2:11). In the latter case, to speak in a tongue (1 Cor 14:4, = to pray in a tongue, 14:14, or to speak with the tongues of angels, 13:1) is a gift of the Spirit (12:10) that

---

[24]J. Panagopoulos, ed., *Prophetic Vocation in the New Testament and Today* (Leiden: Brill, 1977); David Hill, *New Testament Prophecy* (Atlanta: John Knox, 1979); M. Eugene Boring, *Sayings of the Risen Jesus: Christian Prophecy in the Synoptic Tradition* (Cambridge: Cambridge University Press, 1982); David E. Aune, *Prophecy in Early Christianity and the Ancient Mediterranean World* (Grand Rapids: Eerdmans, 1983).

is intelligible only to God unless interpreted (14:15-19) and that is controllable, so that no state of trance, frenzy, or loss of control is involved (14:27-28).

The question of parallels to these phenomena is exceedingly difficult. Most alleged parallels do not carry conviction.[25] From the pagan world the only possible analogy to xenolalia, to my knowledge, is Herodotus, *Histories* 8:135, where the diviner in the temple of Ptoan Apollo speaks in a "foreign language" to Mys of Europa who had come to consult him. Possible analogies to glossolalia are found in Quintilian (*Instituto Oratorio* 1:35) where mention is made of the "more unusual voices of the more secret language which the Greeks call 'glossai' "; in Dio Chrysostom's *10th Discourse on Servants*, where he speaks of the language of the gods and hints at sham glossolalia in referring to "persons who know or three Persian, Median, or Assyrian words and thus fool the ignorant"; and in Lucian's *Alexander* where he says the false prophet uttered "unintelligible vocables which sound like Hebrew or Phoenician" (cf. Celsus in Origen, *Against Celsus* 7:9).

From the Jewish world instances of xenolalia are unknown to me. The most persuasive instance of glossolalia is found in Testament of Job 48-52, where Job's three daughters speak in the angelic language, praising God separately and together in the exalted dialect. In two places the Babylonian Talmud says that Rabbi Johanan ben Zakkai understood not only Torah but also the language of the ministering angels and the matters of the throne chariot of Ezekiel 1 (b Baba Barthra 134a; b. Sukkah 28a).

In the patristic period xenolalia is also difficult to discover. References to glossolalia, however, are to be found easily. In the Ascension of Isaiah 8, we hear that as Isaiah was taken up into the heaven, when he reached the sixth heaven he "praised along with them (the angels) . . . and our praise was like theirs." Irenaeus, *Against Heresies* 5:6:1, tells of Christians "who have received the Spirit of God, and who through the Spirit of God do speak in all languages, as he (Paul) himself also used to speak. In like manner we do also hear many brethren in the church . . . who through the Spirit speak all kinds of languages." Tertullian, *Against Marcion* 5:8, deals with the gifts of the Spirit and assumes that tongues and interpretation of tongues occur in the mainstream church.[26] Viewed in the context of the four types of prayer in as-

---

[25]E. R. Dodds, "Supernormal Phenomena in Classical Antiquity," in *The Ancient Concept of Progress* (Oxford: Clarendon, 1973) 156-210; S. D. Currie, "Speaking in Tongues: Early Evidence Outside the New Testament Bearing on 'Glossais Lalein'," *Int* 19 (1965) 274-94; R. A. Harrisville, "Speaking in Tongues: A Lexicographical Study," *CBQ* 38 (1976) 35-48; David Christie-Murray, *Voices from the Gods: Speaking in Tongues* (London: Routledge & Kegan Paul, 1978); Morton T. Kelsey, *Tongue Speaking: The History and Meaning of Charismatic Experience* (New York: Crossroad, 1981).

[26]For the later Christian history, see Kelsey and Christie-Murray.

cetic theology (meditation, contemplation, mystical union, ecstasy), glossolalia is one kind of contemplative prayer. Like the other kinds of contemplative
prayer, and prophecy, glossolalia has analogues in other traditions. What
makes it Christian, from Paul's perspective, is its source (the Holy Spirit), its
locale (it occurs in a community making the confession, Jesus is Lord, 12:3),
and its results (it edifies the individual Christian who prays this way, 14:4;
when interpreted, it may benefit the church, 14:5, 13).

Following the first Corinthian assertion and Pauline response (14:21-25)
is a concluding summary (14:26-34a) whose thesis is: "Let all things be done
for edification" (14:26b) in public worship. Two things are necessary if this is
to be the case. First, what is said must be capable of being understood by all.
"If anyone speak in a tongue . . . , let one interpret. But if there is no one to
interpret, let each of them keep silence *in church*[27] and speak to himself and
to God" (14:27-28). Second, everything should be done in order. "Let two or
three prophets speak, and let the others weigh what is said. If a revelation is
made to another sitting by, let the first be silent. For you can call all prophesy
one by one, so that all may learn and be encouraged" (14:29-31). Just as with
tongues (14:28), Paul believes prophecy, although a gift/happening, is controllable: "and thus the spirits of prophets are subject to prophets" (14:32).
Although this could conceivably mean that one prophet is subject to the discernment of another prophet (a point made already in 14:29), the context favors
interpreting Paul's language to mean that prophecy is not accompanied by a
trance. 14:33 continues the argument for order in corporate worship: "For God
is not a God of confusion but of peace, as in all the churches of the saints" (cf.
4:17 and 11:16 where the appeal to general practice concludes Paul's argument; so here also, contra RSV, TEV, NIV, NEB, etc.).

The chapter concludes (14:34-40) with a second Corinthian assertion
(14:34-35) and the apostolic response (14:36), followed by a summary (14:37-
40). A group of Corinthian men are quoted:[28] "The women should keep silence in the churches. For they are not permitted to speak, but should be subordinate, as even the law says. If there is anything they desire to know, let them
ask their husbands at home. For it is shameful for a woman to speak in church"
(14:34-35). Paul's reply is indignant: "(Are you saying) either that the word

---

[27]Arnold Bittlinger, *Gifts and Graces*, 102, rightly observes that Paul's critical comments
are directed against uninterpreted speaking in tongues in public, not against the use of tongues
in private devotions.

[28]N. M. Flanagan and E. H. Snyder, "Did Paul Put Down Women in 1 Cor 14:34-36?" *Bib
Theol Bull* 11 (1981) 10-12; D. W. Odell-Scott, "Let the Women Speak in Church: An Egali-
tarian Interpretation of 1 Cor 14:33b-36," *Bib Theol Bull* 13 (1983) 90-93. It is noteworthy that
the Montgomery translation of the New Testament, early in the century, regarded 14:34-35 as a
quote taken from the Corinthian letter to Paul, not Paul's own point of view.

of God originated with you or that it has come to you fellows only?" (14:36)
Two arguments make such a reading probable. First, in vs. 36 the term translated "only" (*monous*) is masculine plural. This requires some such para-
phrase as "you fellows only." If 14:34-35 is Paul's injunction, this masculine
reference is out of place. If 14:34-35 is the argument of a group of males in
the Corinthian community, the masculine reference makes good sense. Second, 14:34-35 is so out of step with Paul's position stated in Gal 3:27-28 and
1 Cor 11:2-16 that any effort to make them fit is contorted, leading often to a
theory of interpolation to get rid of the contradiction.[29] Taking 14:34-35 as a
Corinthian assertion and 14:36 as Paul's indignant response yields a coherent
position with reference to women in Paul's genuine letters.

If one grants the unity of the historical Paul's attitude towards women in
the church, there still remains the problem of the stance of his school, as reflected in 1 Tim 2:11-12: "Let a woman learn in silence with all submissive-
ness. I permit no woman to teach or to have authority over men; she is to keep
silent." The general rule to follow in such ethical matters is twofold: (a) look
at the entire range of New Testament evidence, not just one text, and (b) examine the historical context out of which the various texts emerge.[30] (a) 1 Tim
2:11-12 needs to be set alongside Act 18:24-28, a text from a document that
also has connection with the Pauline school near the end of the first century.
If the Pastorals prohibit a woman's teaching or having authority over men,
Acts 18:26 says Priscilla and Aquila expounded to Apollos the way of God
more accurately. The latter passage not only has a woman teaching a male
preacher but also listed in the dominant role (cf. Acts 13:2, Barnabas and Saul;
13:13, Paul and his company; where the shift in whose names goes first is a
sign of who is the dominant figure in the relationship).[31] Why would two deutero-Pauline documents differ so radically on the function of women in the
church? (b) The Pastorals reflect a situation in which Gnosticism is infecting
the church and is making inroads especially among the women (2 Tim 3:6-7,
"For among the are those who make their way into households and capture

---

[29]For example, Eduard Schweizer, "An Exposition of 1 Cor 14," in *Neotestamentica* (Zu-
rich: Zwingli Verlag, 1963) 333-43, esp. 336.

[30]Brevard Childs, "Biblical Theology's Role in Decision-Making," in *Biblical Theology
in Crisis* (Philadelphia: Westminster, 1970) 123-38; a position approved by Bruce C. Birch and
Larry L. Rasmussen, *Bible and Ethics in the Christian Life* (Minneapolis: Augsburg Publishing
House, 1976).

[31]Textual critics have spotted an antifeminist tendency in the Western text of Acts. Indeed,
there is speculation on the basis of Chrysostom's text of Acts 18:26 (Priscilla expounded to
Apollos the way of the Lord more accurately) that even the oldest and best manuscripts may not
have escaped this touching up. Ben Witherington, "The Anti-feminist Tendencies of the 'Western' Text in Acts," *JBL* 103 (1984) 82-84. Our case does not rest on the legitimacy of such speculation, however.

weak women, burdened with sins and swayed by various impulses, who will listen to anybody and can never arrive at a knowledge of the truth").[32] As a defense against error, the author of the Pastorals appeals to a principle of succession. The true tradition was passed from God to Paul and from the apostle to Timothy and Titus and from them to the faithful men who will teach others also (2 Tim 1:11-12, 13-14; 2:2). It is the author's belief that if the faithful men (obviously the church officials for whom qualifications are given in 1 Tim 3:1-7—see 3:2, "an apt teacher") properly teach the true tradition, then heresy will be defeated. In such a context, the defense of the tradition would not be committed to those most swayed by heresy (the women). Such people would rather be prohibited from exercising authority and from teaching. On the other hand, in Acts Priscilla and Aquila represent the true Pauline tradition that completes a deficient faith or theology. In this context where the woman is a representative of the true tradition there is no reluctance to depict her as the teacher of a male preacher. The constant in the two cases is the faithfulness to the true tradition of Paul. What is variable is how that faithfulness is insured. In one case it is by the exclusion of women from teaching; in the other it is by the inclusion of women in the act of teaching. Such an observation precludes taking 1 Tim 2:11-12 as timeless truth.

Following the second Corinthian assertion (14:34-35) and Paul's reply (14:36), there comes the final summary (14:37-40) at the end of the entire argument. It has two components. There is first of all an assertion of apostolic authority: "If any one thinks that he is a prophet, or spiritual, he should acknowledge that what I am writing to you is a command of the Lord. If any one does not recognize this, he is not recognized" (14:37-38). Presumably this covers Paul's directives in the entire thought unit (1 Cor 12-14). He then reiterates his positions: (a) earnestly desire to prophesy; (b) do not forbid speaking in tongues; (c) do all things decently and in order (14:39).

Having traced the train of thought in 1 Cor 12-14, it is now necessary to attempt to formulate briefly the positions of the two sides, the Corinthians and Paul. On the one hand, the Corinthian spirituals (1) contended that some gifts were better than others; (2) indicated that they wanted the higher gifts; (3) took the position that tongues were for a sign to unbelievers, prophecy for believers; and (4) held that women should not occupy a leadership role in Christian worship. On the other hand, the apostle (1) argued that there are a variety of gifts and each one makes its own contribution to the common good; (2) showed love

---

[32]Martin Dibelius and Hans Conzelmann, *The Pastoral Epistles* (Philadelphia: Fortress, 1972) 116.

to be the indispensable motivation for the manifesting of any gift; (3) insisted that understandable speech is mandatory in corporate worship for both believer and unbeliever; and (4) stood firm for the principle that Christian corporate worship is not a male-dominated enterprise.